DO BLACK LIVES MATTER TO GOD?

Black Characters of Purpose in Scripture

Dr. Jefferson D. Edwards

URIEL PRESS

FIRST URIEL PRESS EDITION

Copyright © 2017 by Dr. Jefferson D. Edwards
www.jeffedwards.org
All rights reserved.

No part of this book may be reproduced or transmitted in any form or by any means, electronic or mechanical, including photocopying, recording, video, or by any information or retrieval system, without prior written permission from the publisher except for the use of brief quotations in a book review.

The author is grateful for permission to use the following copyrighted material: *All the Men of the Bible*, by Herbert Lockyer, copyright 1958. Used by permission of Zondervan, a divison of HarperCollins Publishers.

Published in the United States by Uriel Press
P.O. Box 436987, Chicago, IL 60643
www.urielpress.com
ISBN 978-0-9993326-0-3 *(paperback)*
ISBN 978-0-9993326-1-0 *(ebook)*

LIBRARY OF CONGRESS CONTROL NUMBER: 2017936612

Cover design by Laura Duffy
Book design by Astrid Lewis Reedy

Printed in the United States of America

Table of Contents

PART I

	Introduction	7
CHAPTER 1	The Origin of the Black Race	9
CHAPTER 2	Cush: "Ethiopia"	13
CHAPTER 3	Black Characters Used as a Standard of Judgment	19
CHAPTER 4	Black Characters Showing God's Way	30
CHAPTER 5	Black Characters Who Became "Eyes" for God's People	48

PART II

	Introduction	65
CHAPTER 6	There Was Always a Mixed Multitude with Israel	67
CHAPTER 7	Black Priests in the Bible	71
CHAPTER 8	Black Leaders in the Bible – Old Testament	84
CHAPTER 9	Black Women in the Bible – Old Testament	102
CHAPTER 10	Summary	122
	About The Author	125
	Bibliography	126
	Suggested Reading	128

PART I

Introduction

This book is a presentation of the thread of black characters in Scripture that added to the overall purpose of God's revelation of Himself to man, and His ultimate redemption of man through Christ Jesus our Lord. Blacks were very much a part of God's revelation of Himself to man, contrary to the lack of inclusion of black people in most of the study of characters in the Bible, and most of the commentaries and publications.

In the Western Hemisphere racism not only permeated our educational systems and society, but it also penetrated our religious systems and unfortunately still does today. It has been said many times that the most segregated time in the United States is on Sunday morning between the hours of 9 AM and 11 AM when Whites go to their church, Blacks go to their church, Hispanics go to their church, Asians go to their church, and on and on.

The religious institutions have not helped the matter: major Christian colleges up through the 1980's did not allow black students to attend their colleges or forbade marriages between black and white students. Even in the modern day Charismatic circles, who were some of the first churches who allowed their congregations to become integrated, these mindsets still prevail. Though integration of many of these congregations was allowed, many of those churches were still reluctant to allow blacks to have places of leadership or decision-making responsibilities. They also still were against any inter-marrying of the different races, and also kept perpetuating the myth that black people were under some curse of Ham.

In this book, I hope to show some of the many black characters in Scripture. Some of these black characters, scholars are aware of, but they have discounted their contributions to the purposes of God in Scripture, and in redemption.

Most of my sources and references will be from the Scriptures and scriptural helps. Other references will only be used to substantiate what I have discovered through my scriptural study and research, over many years of ministry.

CHAPTER I

The Origin of the Black Race (Or People of Color)

Ancient Ethiopia (Cush) was the cradle of the Black race or dark-skinned people.

> "And a river went out of Eden to water the garden; and from thence it was parted, and became into four heads. The name of the first is Pison: that is it which compasseth the whole land of Havilah, where there is gold; And the gold of that land is good: there is bdellium and the onyx stone. And the name of the second river is Gihon: the same is it that compasseth the whole land of Ethiopia. And the name of the third river is Hiddekel: that is it which goeth toward the east of Assyria. And the fourth river is Euphrates And the Lord God took the man, and put him into the garden of Eden to dress it and to keep it" (Genesis 2:10–15).

One of the first regions or lands that are mentioned in Scripture is the "…land of Ethiopia," or the lands of Cush. This was not just some incidental nation or land. This land had significant importance in the Bible, and the people of this land had even more of a significant role in relation to God manifesting Himself to man.

Before we can study more specifically Ethiopia or Cush, we must first trace his lineage in Scripture that begins with his father Ham, the son of Noah.

> "And the sons of Noah, that went forth of the ark, were Shem, and Ham, and Japheth and Ham is the father of Canaan. These are the three sons of Noah: and of them was the whole earth overspread. And Noah began to be an husbandman, and he planted a vineyard: And he drank of the wine and was drunken; and he was uncovered within his tent. And Ham, the father of Canaan, saw the nakedness of his father, and told his two brethren without. And Shem and Japheth took a garment, and laid it upon both their shoulders, and went backward, and covered the nakedness of their father; and their faces were backward, and they saw not their father's nakedness. And Noah awoke from his wine, and knew what his younger son had done unto him. And he said, Cursed be Canaan *(notice it was a curse on Canaan, and not on Ham, and there was nothing generational about that curse, and it was not from God, but from Noah who just woke from his wine)*; a servant of servants shall he be unto his brethren. And he said, Blessed be the Lord God of Shem; and Canaan shall be his servant. God shall enlarge Japheth, and he shall dwell in the tents of Shem; and Canaan shall be his servant. And Noah lived after the flood three hundred and fifty years. And all the days of Noah were nine hundred and fifty years: and he died" (Genesis 9:18–29).

"Ham means hot or dark, colored, swarthy. He was the youngest son of Noah and father of Canaan and founder of many peoples (see Genesis 5:32; 6:10; 7:13; 9:18, 22; Psalm 78:51)."[1] "The Hebrew word for Ham means "hot" and is surely prophetic of the climates that have created the blackness of skin of the Negro and the dark complexions of other peoples from the same stock. Egypt is called the land of Ham (Psalm 105:23) and the Egyptian word for "Ham" is "Kem," meaning black and warm. From Ham, we have the Egyptians, Africans, Babylonians, Philistines, Canaanites"[2] and Mongolians (most slanted-eyed people).

"The indignation of Noah found expression in the thrice repeated curse upon Canaan, one of Ham's sons (Genesis 9:25–27). Ham himself suffered in failing to receive the blessing pronounced on his brothers, Shem and Japheth. The peoples polluted by Ham's sin (Genesis 10:15–19) inhabited the land later promised to Abraham's seed; thus the curse of servitude was fulfilled in Joshua's conquest of the Canaanites when he made them hewers of wood and drawers of water (Joshua 9:23, 27)."[3] As stated earlier, there was nothing generational about Noah's curse, for he was not God.

> "And the sons of Ham: Cush, and Mizraim, and Phut, and Canaan. And the sons of Cush; Seba, and Havilah, and Sabtah, and Raaham, and Sabtechah: and the sons of Raamah; Seba and Dedan. And Cush begat Nimrod: he began to be a mighty one in the earth. He was a mighty hunter before the Lord: wherefore it is said, Even as Nimrod the mighty hunter before the Lord. And the beginning of his kingdom was Babel, and Erech, and Accad, and Calneh, in the land of Shinar. Out of that land went forth Asshur, and builded Nineveh, and the city Rehoboth and Calah, and Resen between Nineveh and Calah: the same is a great city" (Genesis 10:6–12).

The following is a brief overview of the four sons of Ham:

"Cush means Black or Ethiopia. He is the eldest son of Ham and founder of a tribal family (Genesis 10:6-8; 1 Chronicles 1:8-10. Cush is also the name of the land where the Cushites dwelt (Isaiah 11:11; 18:1). Cushite is translated Ethiopian."[4]

"Mizraim means Tribulations. He is the 2nd son of Ham and father of Ludim whose descendants were found in Egypt (Genesis 10:6, 13; 1 Chronicles 1:8-11)."[5]

"Phut or Put means Brow or Extension. He is the 3rd son of Ham (Genesis 10:6; I Chronicles 1:8), whose dwelling was in Lybia (Ezekiel 27:10) and whose descendants became hired servants of the Syrians (Nahum 3:9)."[6]

Canaan means Lowland or Trader. He is the youngest son of Ham (Genesis 9:18-27; 1 Chronicles 1:8, 13). He is the founder of the families of the Canaanites (Genesis 10:18). Canaan is also the name of the country in which they dwelt (Genesis 11:31).[7]

---

1 Lockyer, Herbert. *All the Men of the Bible*, p. 134.
2 *Ibid.*
3 *Ibid.*
4 *Ibid.*, p. 86.
5 *Ibid.*, p. 244.
6 *Ibid.*, p. 278.
7 *Ibid.*, p. 83.

CHAPTER 2

Cush: "Ethiopia"

"Cush was the firstborn of Ham; his sons were Havilah, Seba, Sabtah, Raamah, Sebtechah and Nimrod. When Jehovah confounded their language at Babylon, Cush gathered his family and moved south into Africa. He settled in northeast Africa, near his brother Mizraim (Egypt).

Cush established an empire extending through China, India, and Afghanistan. (The word India means black; the Hindu Kush (Cush) Mountains were anciently named by the Black children of "Cush." The Ethiopians controlled those regions for ages, and to this very day, the dwellers of those lands retain the old Ethiopian religious symbols, fine art, and concepts of science, medicine, and engineering. The original architectural structures and municipalities were modified and sometimes mutilated but never destroyed.

The ancient Ethiopians fought continuous wars with the Egyptians, Persians, Hebrews, Assyrians, Arabians and Greeks. The military conqueror Alexander the Great felt Cush's might in 332 B.C. After conquering Egypt easily, the Greek decided to devastate the Ethiopians. During that adventure, Alexander suffered grief and aggravation, as Cush forced his once unconquerable army to retreat to Egypt. Even Rome, in all her glory, was incapable of conquering the Mighty Cush (Jeremiah 46:9). Cush around 25 B.C. defeated Augustus Caesar. He, like Alexander, realized Ethiopia's military proficiency, withdrew his forces and made no other effort to venture south of Egypt's border. Thus, Rome's empire was contained at the northern border of Ethiopia.

During the early nineteen hundreds only Ethiopia and Liberia, out of 47 African nations, were free of white (Japhite) colonialism. However, Liberia was virtually a subsidiary of the Firestone Company. Therefore, Ethiopia was left as the last African independent nation.

In the 20th century, Ethiopia under the rule of Menelik II and Haile Selassie, both of whom boasted direct descendancy from the Ethiopian Queen of Sheba, named Makeda, and King Solomon, electrified the world by twice defeating Italy's large fleet of fighter planes, bombers and cannons, with only mind, muscle and obsolete weapons. This Biblical land of Cush, developed long before Rome was drawn on the map, had once again passed the test of battle.

Ethiopia is the world's oldest Christian country and Africa's oldest free nation. It is the oldest monarchy known to the history of man, having maintained a monarch for some 3000 years. For Cush (Ethiopia) was a great nation before the first book of the Bible was written, as it has been during and after the Biblical recordation period.

The offspring of Cush led civilizations for thousands of years that claimed development in arts, sciences, and public works, while Asia and China were barbaric, London and Paris were swamp lands, and Athens and Rome were vacant sites."[1]

Covenantal Implications of the Ethiopians

The first nation to receive the gospel of the Kingdom of God beyond the Israelites, and the half Jews, Samaria, was Ethiopia. Why did the Ethiopian Eunuch in Acts 8 have the Law of Moses? What was the covenantal purpose and history of the gospel going to this Ethiopian Eunuch whose lineage is from Cush, the originator of the Black race? Let's answer.

Jethro (also called Raguel or Hobab) was the father-in-law of Moses. He was an Ethiopian or Kenite (which is a faction of the Ethiopians) who was a priest serving the Most High God. Moses was married to his Ethiopian daughter, Zipporah, (Numbers 12:1). He served under Jethro and his daughter as an assistant Shepherd in the land of Midian (Exodus 2:15–22; 3:1). Moses entered into a covenant with the nation of the Kenites (Ethiopians).

> "And Moses said unto Hobab, the son of Raguel the Midianite, Moses Father in law, We are journeying unto the place of which the Lord said, I will give it you: come thou with us, and we will do thee good: for the Lord hath spoken good concerning Israel. And he said unto him, I will not go; but I will depart to mine own land, and to my kindred. And he said, Leave us not, I pray thee; forasmuch as thou knowest how we are to encamp in the wilderness, and thou mayest be to us, instead of eyes. And it shall be, if thou go with us, yea, it shall be, that what goodness the Lord shall do unto us, the same will we do unto thee. And they *(Israel and the Kenites)* departed from the mount of the Lord three days' journey: and the ark of the covenant of the Lord went before them in the three days' journey, to search out a resting place for them" (Numbers 10:29–33).

God told Moses that He would be with his mouth, that Aaron would be his spokesman unto the people and that he would be to him instead of a mouth, but Moses would be to him instead of God (See Exodus 4:10–16). So Moses made a covenant with the nation of the Kenites (Ethiopians) and his word was binding as God. He asked them to go with them to the land of promise as scouts and be their "eyes in the wilderness." These Ethiopians (Kenites) were offered the same promises as the Israelites. Moses made a covenant that God would do them good as he did to Israel.

So the Ethiopians (Kenites) were right there with the Jews and entered into the same promises as the children of Israel, which is why they are listed in the Chronicles of Israel in 1 Chronicles 2:55. They dwelt among the royal tribe of Judah and were a part of the life of Israel. They were a much-honored tribe. Of course, they had held a place of honor since Moses was married to Zipporah, an Ethiopian woman and Moses' teacher, and father-in-law was Jethro, an Ethiopian (Kenite) priest.

In the Book of Isaiah, the unique redemptive relationship of Ethiopia (Cush), and Seba, his son, and Egypt (Mizraim) his brother, all descendants of Ham, is seen.

> "But thus saith the Lord that created thee, O Jacob, and he that formed thee, O Israel, Fear not: for I have redeemed thee, I have called thee by thy name; thou are mine. When thou passest through the waters, I will be with thee; and through the rivers, they shall not overflow thee; when thou walkest through the fire, thou shalt not be burned; neither shall the flame kindle upon thee. For I am the Lord thy God, the Holy One of Israel, thy Saviour: I gave Egypt for thy ransom, Ethiopia and Seba for thee. Since thou wast precious in my sight, thou hast been honorable, and I have loved thee: therefore will I give men for thee, and people for thy life" (Isaiah 43:1–4).

The word "ransom" means a cover, that is (literally) a village (as covered in); (specifically) bitumen (as used for coating), and the henna plant (as used for dyeing); figuratively a redemption-price. Some other English transliterations of this Hebrew word are bribe, camp, hire, pitch, satisfaction, sum of money, village. "Ransom" comes from a root word that means to cover (specifically with bitumen); figuratively to expiate or condone, to placate or cancel. Some other English transliterations of this Hebrew root word are appease, make (an) atonement, cleanse, disannul, forgive, be merciful, pacify, pardon, purge (away), put off, (make) reconcile (-iation).[2]

In other words, Ethiopia (Cush) and these other black descendants of Ham were a covering for Israel in the wilderness. Israel was not a strong nation with armies and military might; they had the fewest number of soldiers of all nations and were just coming out of bondage. However, the Ethiopians were known as great and mighty warriors who dwelt in the wilderness. They became an atonement or bribe for the inhabitants of the land to leave Israel alone in their journeys, as long as these black people were with them. They were as a covering village or appeasement to the people in the land. The Ethiopian's literal presence with Israel as a respected people made reconciliation with the other nations in the lands of their journeying. They had come into covenant with Israel and truly became "eyes to them in the wilderness" as well as protection.

We will see that this is the role that many black people and people of color fulfilled in Scripture. In many places in society and history, blacks have also filled the role to do what other ethnic groups seemingly couldn't do – from working the cotton fields of the South in the USA to working the sugar cane fields in the Caribbean Islands to mining the gold and diamond mines in Africa. Many modern inventions that changed modernized society came from this same ethnic group – from central air conditioning to running water in pipes.

In many of the wildernesses of life, it has been black people who have conquered the wilderness and forged a path for others to benefit from.

---

1 Johnson, John L. *The Black Biblical Heritage*, p. 23, 24.
2 Strong, James H. *Strong's Exhaustive Concordance*.

CHAPTER 3

Black Characters Used as a Standard of Judgment

In the Scriptures, many references are made to black characters, nations, and families as a standard to judge the disobedience and religious hypocrisy of Israel, and present a standard of judgment to establish a standard of righteousness.

In Psalm 72, the king is asking for a restoration of righteousness by giving the king and the king's son God's judgments and His righteousness so the people can be judged with righteousness and the poor with judgment. In the middle of that Psalm as part of the restorative process, a prophecy concerning some descendants of Cush are mentioned. "The kings of Tarshish and of the isles shall bring presents: the kings of Sheba and Seba shall offer gifts" (Psalm 72:10). Sheba and Seba are both descendants of Cush or Ethiopia. They are black or dark-skinned people.

In the restoration of the Tabernacle of David, God is restoring not only the tabernacle but proper relationships of Jews and Gentiles with God and one another.

"In that day will I raise up the tabernacle of David that is fallen, and close up the breaches thereof; and I will raise up his ruins, and I will build it as in the days of old: That they may possess the remnant of Edom, and of all the heathen, which are called by my name, saith the Lord that doeth this," (Amos 9:11, 12).

The remnant or residue of Edom refers to Esau, who through his union or marriage to a Hittite and an Egyptian (both black descendants of Ham), formed the nation of Edom. I will give greater detail to this when I trace the roots of Caleb. However, this passage in Amos is quoted or referred to when the Apostle James who was over the Jerusalem or mother church, had a great fight concerning the gentiles coming into Christianity. Many Jews wanted the Gentiles to be circumcised or become Jews before they could receive salvation in Jesus Christ. To settle this issue, the Apostle James said:

"...Men and brethren, hearken unto me: Simeon hath declared how God at the first did visit the Gentiles, to take out of them a people for His name. And to this agree the words of the prophets; as it is written, After this I will return (overturn) and will build again the tabernacle of David, which is fallen down; and I will build again the ruins thereof, and I will set it up: That the residue of men might seek after the Lord, and all the Gentiles, upon whom my name is called, saith the Lord who doeth all these things. Known unto God are all his works from the beginning of the world. Wherefore my sentence is, that we trouble not them, which from among the Gentiles are turned to God:"
(Acts 15:14–18).

At Zion, which is a spiritual dimension of the church, as well as the highest mountain in Jerusalem (the city of righteousness, the city of peace), there was the tabernacle of David, as well as the throne of David. Here, at Mt. Zion was a function of the Melchizedek order of priesthood because there was not a Levitical order that

Black Characters Used as a Standard of Judgment

emanated from the Law given to Israel that was functioning when the ark was restored to Israel. Neither did the law allow David, from the tribe of Judah to set up the ark. Even Obededom (which we'll look at later) a Gentile, and his family served as doorkeepers and porters in the tabernacle, after the Ark of the Covenant had been in their house for three months. It is mentioned about Zion, that: "The Lord loveth the gates of Zion more than all the dwellings of Jacob. Glorious things are spoken of thee, O city of God. Selah. I will make mention of Rahab and Babylon to them that know me: behold Philistia, and Tyre with Ethiopia; this man was born there. And of Zion it shall be said, This and that man was born in her: and the highest himself shall establish her. The Lord shall count, when he writeth up the people, that this man was born there. Selah" (Psalm 87:2–6). These are all descendants of Ham and his son Cush (Ethiopia). They were all black or dark-skinned people.

In the gospels, descendants of this same nation (Ethiopia) are used to judge the religious hypocrisy and presenting a standard of judgment to establish righteousness. In Luke 11: 14–23, Jesus began dealing with the religious order of that day who wanted a "sign from heaven." He dealt with their refusal to receive Him totally, and He dealt with their hypocrisy. They accused Him of being a devil, and they refused to accept the true kingdom of God and the principles related to it, namely, righteousness, which is right standing with God and right standing with one another.

> "And when the people were gathered thick together, he began to say, This is an evil generation" they seek a sign; and there shall no sign be given it, but the sign of Jonas the prophet. For as Jonas was a sign unto the Ninevites, so shall also the Son of man be to this generation. The queen of the south shall rise up in the judgment with the men of this generation, and condemn them: for she came from the utmost parts of the earth to hear the

wisdom of Solomon; and, behold, a greater than Solomon is here. The men of Nineveh shall rise up in the judgment with this generation, and shall condemn it: for they repented at the preaching of Jonas; and, behold, a greater than Jonas is here" (Luke 11:29–32).

Jesus took the example of an Old Testament prophet and two black nations to exemplify judgment against the unrighteousness of this generation and their religious system. First of all the sign of Jonah the prophet, not only concerning this cameo of being in the belly of the fish, foreshadowing Jesus being in the belly of the earth for three days, but also a sign for this evil generation. The sign of Jonah:

1) You can't escape God.
2) God only speaks to you to repent.
3) Mercy is available to those who will repent

Then Jesus mentions the Ninevites or the Men of Nineveh. The gospel says the men of Nineveh (or lineage of Nineveh) shall rise up in the judgment or as a standard with this generation. 1 Peter 4:17 says, "…judgment must begin at the house of God…" This is judgment in whether you obey the gospel or not. This gospel of the Kingdom (righteousness) must be preached as a witness (evidential lifestyle or something evidential), to every race (nation). Jesus said they repented at the preaching of Jonah. This speaks of a generation (or religious order) that won't change and won't repent.

The Ninevites lineage trace back to Ham, Cush, and Nimrod (see Genesis 9:18, 19; Genesis 10:6–12). "Nineveh was a cruel nation; history says they made a temple out of the skulls of conquered soldiers."[1] However, God sent a prophet to this heathen nation because of their connection to Cush, or the Ethiopians and an end-time destiny that's mentioned in the gospels. The inhabitants of Nineveh were a dark-skinned people.

Then Jesus mentions the "...Queen of South..." (Luke 11:31), who is from Sheba, which was originally a part of Ethiopia (Cush). "Her name is Makeda."[2] Her lineage is traced back to Cush and Seba and Sheba (see Genesis 10:7).

Jesus goes on to say, "the ...Queen of the South (Makeda)... shall rise up in judgment with the men of this generation..." (Luke 11:31). This is a generation that refuses to accept totally the gospel of the Kingdom (Righteousness). She was a dark-skinned or Ethiopian woman.

Other Characters Used As A Standard

God has used a dark-skinned people throughout the history of Israel and in the scriptures to judge the disobedience and rebellion of Israel.

Rechab or The Rechabites

Rechab or The Rechabites were a Kenite or Ethiopian family. He was a descendant of Hemath, a Kenite. "And the families of the scribes which dwelt at Jabez; the Tirathites, the Shimeathites, and Suchathites. These are the Kenites that came of Hemath, the father of the house of Rechab" (1 Chronicles 2:55). He was also the father of Jehonadab and founder of a tribe known as the "Rechabites." "And when he (Jehu) was departed thence, he lighted on Jehonadab, the son of Rechab coming to meet him: and he saluted him, and said to him, Is thine heart right, as my heart is with thy heart? And Jehonadab answered, It is. If it be, give me thine hand; and he took him up to him into the chariot. And he said, Come with me, and see my zeal for the Lord. So they made him ride in his chariot" (2 Kings 10:15, 16). Jehu took this man, Jehonadab to be a witness when he destroyed the descendants of Ahab and the Baal worshippers.

> "And Jehu went, and Jehonadab the son of Rechab, into the house of Baal, and said unto the worshippers of Baal, search, and look that there be here with you none of the servants of the Lord, but the worshippers of Baal only. And when they went in to offer sacrifices and burnt offerings, Jehu appointed fourscore men without, and said, If any of the men whom I have brought into your hands escape, he that letteth him go, his life shall be for the life of him. And it came to pass, as soon as he had made an end of offering the burnt offering that Jehu said to the guard and to the captains, Go in, and slay them; let none come forth. And they smote them with the edge of the sword; and the guard and the captain cast them out, and went to the city of the house of Baal. And they brought forth the images out of the house of Baal, and burned them. And they brake down the image of Baal, and brake down the house of Baal, and made it a draught house unto this day. Thus Jehu destroyed Baal out of Israel" (2 Kings 10:15, 23–28).

These Rechabites were a standard that God used to judge Judah. They were a continuation of the picture or lineage of Ethiopians becoming a standard of judgment to bring reconciliation and righteousness.

Rehab's name means, rider or charioteer. It comes from a root word, which means to ride (on an animal or in a vehicle): to place upon (for riding or general), to dispatch. Some of the other English words transliterated from this Hebrew word include bring (on [horse-] back), carry, get [oneself] up on [horse-] back, put, (cease to, make to) ride (in a chariot, on, -r), set.³

"The word which came unto Jeremiah from the Lord in the days of Jehoiakim the son of Josiah king of Judah, saying, Go unto the house of the Rechabites, and speak unto them, and bring them into the house of the Lord, into one of the chambers, and give them wine to drink. Then I took Jaazaniah the son of Jeremiah, the son of Habaziniah, and his brethren, and all his sons, and the whole house of the Rechabites; And I brought them into the house of the Lord, into the chamber of the sons of Hanan, the son of Igdaliah, a man of God, which was by the chamber of the princes, which was above the chamber of Maaseiah the son of Shallum, the keeper of the door. And I set before the sons of the house of the Rechabites pots full of wine, and cups, and I said unto them, Drink ye wine. But they said, We will drink no wine: for Jonadab the son of Rechab our father commanded us, saying, Ye shall drink no wine, neither ye, nor your sons for ever: Neither shall ye build house, nor sow seed, nor plant vineyard, nor have any: but all your days ye shall dwell in tents; that ye many live many days in the land where ye be strangers. Thus have we obeyed the voice of Jonadab the son of Rechab our father in all that he hath charged us, to drink no wine all our days, we, our wives, our sons, nor our daughters; Nor to build houses for us to dwell in: neither have we vineyard, nor field, nor seed: But we have dwelt in tents, and have obeyed, and done according to all that Jonadab our father commanded us. But it came to pass, when Nebuchadnezzar king of Babylon came up into the land, that we said, Come, and let us go to Jerusalem for fear of the army of the Chaldeans, and for fear of the army of the Syrians: so we dwelt at Jerusalem" (Jeremiah 35:1–11).

"Rechab's name also means championship, a horseman, or square. He was a man who vowed to be separate. This particular order had its rise in the religious revival that took place under Elijah the prophet, and Elisha the prophet. The tenets of the followers of Rechab were a reaction and a protest against the luxury and license which under Jezebel and Ahab threatened to destroy the simplicity of the ancient nomadic life of Israel.

Accordingly, the Rechabites vowed to drink no wine, nor build houses, nor sow seed, nor plant vineyards, but dwell in tents all their days. They were to remember they were strangers in the land. For 250 years they adhered faithfully to their rules but were driven from their tents when in 607 B. C. Nebuchadnezzar invaded Judah.

Of these noteworthy people, whose high moral example was specially commended by God, Dr. Dinsdale Young elaborates on these points:

1) They honored the memory of the good.
2) They were marked by great simplicity of life.
3) They were worshippers of Jehovah.
4) They maintained their integrity amid surrounding degeneracy.
5) They had their principles severely tested.
6) They received a special blessing."[4]

> "Then came the word of the Lord unto Jeremiah, saying, Thus saith the Lord of hosts, the God of Israel; Go and tell the men of Judah and the inhabitants of Jerusalem, Will ye not receive instruction to hearken to my words? saith the Lord. The words of Jonadab the son of Rechab, that he commanded his sons not to drink wine, are performed; for unto this day they drink none, but obey their father's commandment: notwithstanding I have spoken unto you, rising early and speaking; but ye hearkened not unto me. I have sent also unto you all my servants the prophets, rising up early and sending them, saying, Return ye now every man from his evil way, and amend your doings, and go not after other

gods to serve them, and ye shall dwell in the land which I have given to you and to your fathers: but ye have not inclined your ear, nor hearkened unto me. Because the sons of Jonadab the son of Rechab have performed the commandment of their father, which he commanded them; but this people hath not hearkened unto me: Therefore thus saith the Lord God of hosts, the God of Israel; Behold, I will bring upon Judah and upon all the inhabitants of Jerusalem all the evil that I have pronounced against them: because I have spoken unto them, but they have not heard; and I have called unto them, but they have not answered" (Jeremiah 35:12–17).

Here God used these black Kenites (Ethiopians) as a standard of obedience to judge the disobedience of the men of Judah. God had sent prophets to these people, admonishing them to return to the Lord and depart from evil and amend their doing and stop serving other gods, but they would not hearken to God. As a result of the Rechabites keeping the commandments of their father Rechab "for over 250 years,"[5] God gave a generational prophecy to the descendants of these black Ethiopian people.

> "And Jeremiah said unto the house of the Rechabites, Thus said the Lord of hosts, the God of Israel; Because ye have obeyed the commandment of Jonadab your father, and kept all his precepts, and done according unto all that he hath commanded you: Therefore thus said the Lord of hosts, the God of Israel; Jonadab the son of Rechab shall not want a man to stand before me forever" (Jeremiah 35:18, 19).

God declared that there "...shall never lack a descendant to stand before me..." (Amplified Bible). In another translation, God said, there "...shall never fail to have a man to serve me..." (New International Version). This is a powerful prophecy that probably even adds to part of the purpose that I, as a black man, and many other black people are serving the Lord with our whole heart and soul today.

The prophetic and covenantal implications of God's word to this black family should be an encouragement to all believers: that God rewards faithfulness and obedience. Throughout periods in the history of the people of God and the Bible, black people have stood before the Lord and served Him based on this prophecy to this black family of the Rechabites. From this lineage of faithful blacks, even in the midst of evil times, have come some of the greatest moves of God that have affected the church.

One of the historic moves, the Azusa Street Movement, affected the church world immensely. This movement which started among black people in Los Angeles, California brought a restoration of the importance of the Holy Spirit's administration back to the church. For a few years, there was a color-blind movement affecting blacks and whites where the blood wiped away division in the United States and over 35 countries abroad.

William Seymour, a black man, was the leader of this movement. Despite the racism and segregation of that time, the Holy Spirit infused his life and made him the leader of a color-blind movement of the Holy Spirit that birthed many church movements. Out of Azusa Street came the Church of God in Christ Churches, the Apostolic Faith Churches, the United Holy Churches, the Assembly of God Churches, the Foursquare Gospel Churches, the United Pentecostal Churches, the Pentecostal Holiness Churches, the Church of God (Cleveland, Tennessee), and the Pentecostal Assemblies of the World, just to name a few.

In my experience, the Lord brought a remnant out of the traditional churches in the black church community and brought many black leaders including myself in the 1980's and 1990's to the forefront of church leadership. Many black men and women led churches that grew to be effective in God's purposes, and some even grew in numbers from several hundred to several thousand. Many black leaders became a part of the church conference circuit, where there had been only white leaders before that time. Many black leaders started becoming best-selling authors in the church world in the 90's and have continued to this day.

There have been black men and women up to the present day standing before the Lord in fulfillment of the prophecy to this black family, the Rechabites.

---

1 Lockyer, Herbert. *All the Men of the Bible*, p. 251.
2 Woolsey, Raymond H. *Men and Women of Color in the Bible*, p. 52.
3 Strong, James. *Strong's Exhaustive Concordance*.
4 Lockyer, Herbert. *All the Men of the Bible*, p. 283.
5 *Ibid.*

CHAPTER 4

Black Characters Showing God's Way

A Black Messenger

Cushi – means the Ethiopian. He brought the right message in the midst of a crisis, at the right time, and in the right way. Absalom, King David's son, plotted to take the kingdom from his father, David. "…Absalom stole the hearts of the men of Israel" (2 Samuel 15:6). He conspired against King David and all his counsel and judgment. When anyone had a controversy against King David's judgment, Absalom would comfort them and turn them against King David. Eventually, Absalom set himself up as king and King David had to flee Jerusalem to escape from Absalom (See 2 Samuel chapters 15–18). After Absalom was eventually killed in battle by Joab, a prophetic event happened involving a black Ethiopian.

> "Then said Ahimaaz the son of Zadok, Let me now run, and bear the king tidings, how that the Lord hath avenged him of his enemies. And Joab said unto him, Thou shalt not bear tidings this

day, but thou shalt bear tidings another day: but this day thou shalt bear no tidings, because the king's son is dead. Then said Joab to Cushi *(the Ethiopian)*, Go tell the king what thou hast seen. And Cushi bowed himself unto Joab, and ran" (2 Samuel 18:19–21).

Since Ahimaaz was the son of Zadok the priest, both being Israelites, it was the custom in Israel to have certain days of mourning for other Israelites, especially the royal family, and during military ventures. Joab told Cushi the Ethiopian to go and tell the news to King David. Cushi was not an Israelite, and it was his appointed time to run with the appropriate message for this particular day. However, Ahimaaz the son of Zadok insisted on running to carry the message even though he had no message and it was not his time. Ahimaaz's name means brother of anger. It comes from a root word that means closure or to fasten (or make firm), that is, to close (the eyes). Another English word that is transliterated from this Hebrew word is **shut**.[1] It also means **a rascal**.[2] Ahimaaz is symbolic of one who is out of time, wants to run with a message, but has no vision because his eyes are not open. Because many people will not see things the way they really are, or they shut their eyes to the truth, especially in relation to racial issues, they have no message from God that brings solutions to the problems at hand.

> "Then said Ahimaaz the son of Zadok yet again to Joab, But howsoever, let me, I pray thee, also run after Cushi. And Joab said, Wherefore wilt thou run, my son, seeing that thou hast no tidings ready? But howsoever, said he, let me run. And he said unto him, Run. Then Ahimaaz ran by the way of the plain *(smooth place)*, and overran Cushi" (2 Samuel 18:22, 23).

Ahimaaz took the easy route, the plain or smooth place, while Cushi took the route over the mountains, so Ahimaaz was able to out run Cushi, getting to the destination or purposed place sooner; however, he had no message when he got there.

Ahimaaz symbolizes some people in life who seem to achieve things or get to places of status quicker than other people. This sometimes happens because of their economic status in life and the privileges that come with that status. However, they may not exemplify the will of God when they get to that place because they lost their vision trying to run, or get to that place of status too easily or too quickly. While Cushi, the black man symbolizes those who had to travel a hard, rocky and tedious journey, but when they get to their destination, if they don't lose their vision, they will have a purposeful message for the times.

> "And David sat between the two gates: and the watchman went up to the roof over the gate unto the wall, and lifted up his eyes, and looked, and behold a man running alone. And the watchman cried, and told the king. And the king said, If he be alone, there is tidings in his mouth. And he came apace, and drew near. And the watchman saw another man running: and the watchman called unto the porter, and said, Behold another man running alone. And the king said, He also bringeth tidings. And the watchman said, me thinketh the running of the foremost is like the running of Ahimaaz the son of Zadok, And the king said, he is a good man, and cometh with good tidings. And Ahimaaz called, and said unto the king, All is well, And he fell down to the earth upon his face before the king, and said, Blessed be the Lord thy God, which hath delivered up the men that lifted up their hand against my lord the king. And the king said, Is the young man Absalom safe? And Ahimaaz answered, When Joab sent the king's servant, and me thy servant, I saw a great tumult, but I knew not what it was. And the king said unto him, Turn aside, and stand here. And he turned aside, and stood still" (2 Samuel 18:24–30).

Ahimaaz not only had no purposeful or present day vision or word, but he also didn't have the courage to speak the hard word. There is sometimes a hard word that needs to be spoken that many might say is not good news or inspirational or some nice word, but it is nonetheless necessary to bring judgment and closure to one season and then open a new season.

> "And, behold, Cushi came; and Cushi said, Tidings, my lord the king: for the Lord hath avenged thee this day of all them that rose up against thee. And the king said unto Cushi, Is the young man Absalom safe? And Cushi answered, The enemies of my lord the king, and all that rise against thee to do thee hurt, be as that young man is" (2 Samuel 18:31, 32).

The message was not a pleasant word but it was a timely word, and it was God's word. There is a destiny for other people of color, just like Cushi, to carry an end time message of judgment putting down divisions, rebellion, and flesh rule, and establishing and bringing a reconstitution of God-ordained order.

I've watched the Lord raise up many black people to deal with hard times when other people had given up or retreated because of present situations in society.

Some of the first emergences of black leaders in recent history came when many of America's urban cities were on the brink of bankruptcy. New black leaders came to the forefront and were elected mayors of cities that were in trouble. Trouble and crisis were not a deterrent to them because that had been their life experiences. This phenomenon was repeated in not only city elections, but also in national elections.

During some of the worst crises, black people who have been seasoned by crisis emerge to challenge the times.

A Black King and Warrior

Shishak – was the King of Egypt. History says that he was originally "a king of Libya who subjugated Egypt and formed a Libyan Dynasty. While in power, he exhibited mercy to Jeroboam by granting him asylum from Solomon. He governed Egypt from 935–914 B.C. Shishak was a black man from the lineage of Ham's third son Phut."[3] "History refers to him as *Sesconchis I,* founder of the twenty-second Bubastic dynasty, who reigned for twenty-one years."[4]

Shishak was used by God to invade Judah, "...because they had transgressed against the Lord" (2 Chronicles 12:2). His army was made up of Egyptians from the lineage of Ham's second son Mizraim. It was also "composed of Libyans and Ethiopians."[5] The Ethiopians, of course, came from Ham's firstborn son Cush. Also with King Shishak's army was the Sukkiims, another group of black people, who were inhabitants of some place near Egypt. Their name means **hut-dwellers**.[6] "Some think these were the Scenite Arabs, dwellers in tents, but others maintain more justly that these were Arab-Troglodytes, who inhabited the caverns of a mountain range on the western coast of the Red Sea."[7] "The Troglodytes, a people of Egypt on the coast of the Red Sea. They were called Troglodytes, 'because they dwelt in caves.' – Hesych."[8]

> "And it came to pass, when Rehoboam had established the kingdom, and had strengthened himself, he forsook the law of the Lord, and all Israel with him. And it came to pass, that in the fifth year of king Rehoboam, Shishak king of Egypt came up against Jerusalem, because they had transgressed against the Lord, With twelve hundred chariots, and threescore thousand horsemen: and the people were without number that came with him out of Egypt; the Lubims (*Libyans)*, the Sukkiims, and the Ethiopians. And he took the fenced cities which pertained to Judah, and came to Jerusalem" (2 Chronicles 12:1–4).

It is important to recognize that these black nations were part of an Empire, referred to as the Egyptian Empire. This empire consisted of three major nations: Egypt, Ethiopia, and Lybia, all coming from Ham's three sons. Egypt was from the lineage of Mizraim, Ethiopia was from the lineage of Cush, and Lybia was from the lineage of Phut. Their assault against Judah was directed by God as punishment for Judah's transgressions against the Lord. God again uses these black nations and people as a standard of judgment concerning His people. Many of these people already had a One-God concept and had a priest who served the Most High God. The Most High God was introduced to Abraham by one of their ancestors, Melchizedek. Abraham had learned to worship and build altars in the land of these black people, who already had a One-God concept. Moses was also introduced to the Most High God through the priest Jethro, another ancestor of this people. Here black people were used as a standard of judgment.

> "Then came Shemaiah the prophet to Rehoboam, and to the princes of Judah, that were gathered together to Jerusalem because of Shishak, and said unto them, Thus said the Lord, Ye have forsaken me, and therefore have I also left you in the hand of Shishak. Whereupon the princes of Israel and the king humbled themselves; and they said, The Lord is righteous. And when the Lord saw that they humbled themselves, the word of the Lord came to Shemaiah, saying, They have humbled themselves, therefore I will not destroy them, but I will grant them some deliverance; and my wrath shall not be poured out upon Jerusalem by the hand of Shishak" (2 Chronicles 12:5–7).

God used Shishak to punish Judah because of their transgressions, and this caused Judah, through the admonishment of the Prophet Shemaiah, to humble themselves and admit to their transgressions. The Lord then did not allow the punishment to elevate to the level of wrath by the hand of Shishak. However, the Lord wanted to keep Judah under the servanthood of Shishak because they were too arrogant and didn't know how to serve. They were to be a nation high in honor, high in praise, high in name above the other nations (See Deuteronomy 26:19). But this was so that eventually, in or through them, that all the nations of the earth might be blessed (see Genesis 12:3). However, they despised any one that was not part of their nation.

These descendants of Ham had an innate ability to serve. God wanted that ability to be imparted to His chosen people, Israel, especially the tribe of Judah, the ruling tribe. They had to learn to serve. So God ordered Judah to be under these descendants of Ham for a period of time to receive impartation by association. Judah was to be their servants to learn how to serve and benefit from their culture. In this situation, the descendants of Ham were used as a standard of service in Scripture.

> "Nevertheless they shall be his servants; that they may know my service, and the service of the kingdoms of the countries. So Shishak king of Egypt came up against Jerusalem, and took away the treasures of the house of the Lord, and the treasures of the king's house; he took all: he carried away also the shields of gold which Solomon had made. And when he (Rehoboam) humbled himself, the wrath of the Lord turned from him, that he would not destroy him altogether: and also in Judah things went well" (2 Chronicles 12:8, 9, 12).

As a descendant of this ethnic group, I have seen throughout history and in my own experience, the propensity of black people and other people of color to serve. We have served in capacities that would have killed other ethnic groups – but too many times in history it was forced service and enslaved service.

This natural gift of service has been exploited by other ethnic groups to benefit their lavish lifestyles. United Kingdom Great Britain exploited the service gift of black people by conquering nations of color across the world, partly motivated by their fear of preservation if they didn't control the people in the majority at that time, which were people of color, that make up 80 to 90% of the world. The only white nations that Great Britain conquered were Ireland and Scotland, for land mass. Every other conquered or colonized nation was a nation of color.

Through the gift of service of these people from the lineage of Ham, European nations along with the USA and Australia have taken the forefront of control of the world by exploiting the labor and service of descendants of Ham.

Even under oppressive regimes, black people have served their oppressors through plagues and diseases that did not affect them. During those times they nursed and buried their oppressors.

This God-given gift that is natural to my lineage has been despised by many black people because of slavery and oppression. However, despite its misuse by others, we must realize that this is one of our gifts from God and reclaim its purpose in God's Kingdom.

A Black Woman Warrior

Jael – was the wife of Heber, the Kenite (Ethiopian). These Kenites (Ethiopians) helped Israel in their journeys in the wilderness. Through a covenant made with Jethro, an Ethiopian (Kenite) priest and father-in-law of Moses, they became scouts or "eyes in the wilderness" for Israel. The Covenant made by Moses was that whatever good that came to Israel would also come to these Ethiopians if they would help them get through the wilderness (See Numbers 10:29–33). They became an essential part of Israel, especially since Moses had married into their tribe, by taking Zipporah, the daughter of Jethro, the Kenite/Ethiopian priest who was serving in Midian, to be his wife.

Israel served the Lord all the days of Joshua, all the days of the elders that outlived Joshua, which had known all the works of the Lord that he had done for Israel (See Joshua 24:31). After Joshua's death, Israel fought against the Canaanites but was not obedient to drive out all the inhabitants of Canaan out of the land. "And the Lord was with Judah; and he drove out the inhabitants of the mountains; but could not drive out the inhabitants of the valley, because they had chariots of iron" (Judges 1:19). The children of Benjamin, of Manasseh, of Ephraim, of Zebulun, of Asher, and of Naphtali, were all disobedient and did not drive out all the Canaanite inhabitants of Jerusalem, and the other lands in Canaan that were given to the tribes of Israel by covenant for an inheritance.

> "And an angel of the Lord came up from Gilgal to Bochim, and said, I made you to go up out of Egypt, and have brought you unto the land which I sware unto your fathers; and I said, I will never break my covenant with you. And ye shall make no league with the inhabitants of this land; ye shall throw down their altars: but ye have not obeyed my voice: why have ye done this? Wherefore I also said, I will not drive them out from before you; but they shall be as thorns in your sides, and their gods shall be a snare unto you" (Judges 2:1–3).

Even though Israel was convicted and wept because of what the angel of the Lord spoke, they didn't repent of their ways. As stated above, they served the Lord all the days of Joshua and all the days of the elders with Joshua, but after Joshua had let every man go unto their inheritance to possess the land, they started doing what was right in their own eyes. When Joshua died, a generation rose up which knew not the Lord, and didn't know the works that the Lord had done for Israel.

> "And the children of Israel did evil in the sight of the Lord, and served Baalim: And they forsook the Lord God of their fathers, which brought them out of the land of Egypt, and followed other gods, of the gods of the people that were round about them, and bowed themselves unto them, and provoked the Lord to anger. And they forsook the Lord and served Baal and Ashtaroth" (Judges 2:11–13).

Because Israel forsook God, He allowed these nations, which happened to be black nations from the lineage of Canaan, Ham's son, to judge or prove Israel whether they would obey the Lord or not. Again black people, even those who were enemies of Israel were used as a standard of judgment against the unrighteousness and disobedience of God's chosen people.

> "And the anger of the Lord was hot against Israel; and he said, Because that this people hath transgressed my covenant which I commanded their fathers, and have not hearkened unto my voice; I will not henceforth drive out any from before them of the nations which Joshua left when he died: That through them I may prove Israel, whether they will keep the way of the Lord to walk therein, as their fathers did keep it, or not. Therefore the Lord left those nations, without driving them out hastily; neither delivered he them into the hand of Joshua" (Judges 2:20–23).

Israel was supposed to be a nation that was high in honor, high in praise, high in name above the other nations that through them all the nations of the earth would be blessed. However, they began to be like the other nations and failed in their witness of Jehovah God to the other nations. Since they choose the gods of those nations rather than Jehovah God Almighty, then God used those nations and their gods to be teachers, standard-bearers, and even taskmasters over Israel. The laws and the lessons of obedience that should have developed character in God's people were rejected, so God used these nations to teach those lessons in a hard way. It has been said that "experience is the best teacher"—but the other side of that is—"only because the fool could learn no other way." It is better to learn by instruction. The Apostle Paul said, "I was instructed of the Lord," but Israel did not use that avenue to learn during this time in history.

> "Now these are the nations which the Lord left, to prove Israel by them, even as many of Israel as had not known all the wars of Canaan; Only that the generations of the children of Israel might know, to teach them war, at the least such as before knew nothing thereof; Namely, five lords of the Philistines, and all the Canaanites, and the Sidonians, and the Hivites that dwelt in mount Lebanon, from mount Baalhermon unto the entering in of Hamath. And they were to prove Israel by them, to know whether they would hearken unto the commandments of the Lord, which he commanded their fathers by the hand of Moses" (Judges 3:1–4).

Jael, the wife of Heber the Kenite (Ethiopian), became an important figure in the life of Israel during this time of war and subjugation to the Canaanites of the land. "And the children of the Kenite (Ethiopian), Moses' father in law, went up out of the city of palm trees (Jericho) with the children of Judah into the wilderness of Judah, which lieth in the south of Arad; and they went and dwelt among the people" (Judges 1:16). Even though the Lord because of

Israel's disobedience allowed the Canaanites to subjugate and oppress them, whenever they cried out to God again, He would raise up judges or champions which delivered them out of the hand of those that distressed them or spoiled them. But they would not hearken unto their judges, but they "...went a whoring after other gods, and bowed themselves unto them..." They were easy to turn away from the Lord and the commandments that their fathers walked in and had taught them. Then again the Lord in His mercy raised up judges to deliver them.

> "And when the Lord raised them up judges, then the Lord was with the Judge, and delivered them out of the hand of their enemies all the days of the judge: for it repented the Lord because of their groanings by reason of them that oppressed them and vexed them. And it came to pass, when the judge was dead, that they returned, and corrupted themselves more than their fathers, in following other gods to serve them, and to bow down unto them; they ceased not from their own doings, nor from their stubborn way" (Judges 2:18, 19).

The children of Israel did this over and over, and God raised up Othniel the son of Kenaz, a black man, who was Caleb's younger brother, and then He raised up Ehud, the son of Gera, a Benjamite, and finally Deborah, a prophetess, the wife of Lapidoth. Because the children of Israel had continuously done evil in the sight of the Lord after Ehud, the judge was dead, the Lord sold Israel into the hand of Jabin, king of Canaan, and Sisera his captain (See Judges 3).

> "And the children of Israel again did evil in the sight of the Lord, when Ehud was dead. And the Lord sold them into the hand of Jabin king of Canaan, that reigned in Hazor; the captain of whose host was Sisera, which dwelt in Harosheth of the Gentiles.

And the children of Israel cried unto the Lord: for he had nine hundred chariots of iron; and twenty years he mightily oppressed the children of Israel. And Deborah, a prophetess, the wife of Lapidoth, she judged Israel at that time" (Judges 4:1–3).

The children of Israel then came up where Deborah, the prophetess dwelt for her judgment concerning Jabin and Sisera. She sent and called Barak the son of Abinoam out of Kedesh-naphtali, and said the Lord had called him to take ten thousand men of the children of Naphtali and Zebulun and that the Lord would draw Sisera, the captain of Jabin's army "…with his chariots and his multitude…" and would deliver them into the hands of Barak. "Then Barak said unto her (Deborah), If thou wilt go with me, then I will go: but if thou wilt not go with me, then I will not go" (Judges 4:8).

Here is the scenario where Deborah has been known as one of the unique women in the Bible that have been greatly used by God. In fact, she is one of the primary women that are used to justify God's use of women in Scripture. She is heralded by many women ministers as a hero and used by many preachers on Mother's Day in the United States to show the virtue of women. She is the only woman that the Bible mentions that was a judge of Israel. She made a very important prophetic proclamation to Barak and to Israel by the mouth of God. "And she said, I will surely go with thee: notwithstanding the journey that thou takest shall not be for thine honour; for the Lord shall sell Sisera into the hand of a woman. And Deborah arose, and went with Barak to Kedesh" (Judges 4:9).

It is because of this prophetic proclamation that Deborah has not only been heralded as a woman prophetess and judge but also as a warrior that lead Barak to defeat the Canaanites under the rule of Jabin the king and his captain Sisera, who had oppressed the children of Israel. However, even though Deborah was used to help defeat the Canaanites, she was not the one who was the fulfillment of this particular prophetic proclamation. The prophecy was that "...the Lord shall sell Sisera into the hand of a woman..." (Judges 4:9). Deborah was not the woman that fulfilled this prophecy. It was a black woman, named Jael who fulfilled this prophecy, but she has gotten very little recognition by theologians, preachers, and teachers, and she has hardly received any recognition as being a black woman, who fulfilled this prophecy given to Deborah, by the hand of God.

> "Now Heber the Kenite (Ethiopian), which was of the children of Hobab the father in law of Moses, had severed himself from the Kenites, and pitched his tent into the plain of Zaanaim, which is by Kedesh" (Judges 4:11).

The Kenites as a people dwelt in the wilderness of Judah, and are listed in the Chronicle of Judah (See 1 Chronicles 2:55). Even though they dwelt in the wilderness of Judah, they stayed very close to Judah as the ruling tribe, in all their affairs. They were a covenant people with Israel and had a very special place in the history of Israel especially in relation to Abraham and Moses. However, Heber the Kenite chose to dwell even further in the wilderness and severed himself from even his wilderness-dwelling people.

Deborah and Barak went up against Sisera under the proclamation of Deborah when she said to Barak, "...Up; for this day in which the Lord hath delivered Sisera into thine hand: is not the Lord gone out before thee...?" (Judges 4:14). The Lord discomfited Sisera and all his chariots and all his host by the edge of the sword before Barak. In our terms they really beat them down -- so much so that Sisera, the captain, got down from his chariot and fled away on his feet. However, Barak kept pursuing after the chariots, and after the host, "...and all the host of Sisera fell upon the edge of the sword; and there was not a man left" (Judges 4:16).

The prophecy of Deborah was that the Lord would sell or deliver Sisera into the hand of a woman. Even though the host of Sisera was defeated and destroyed, Sisera had not been destroyed. This is where the fulfillment of the prophecy came to pass.

> "Howbeit Sisera fled away on his feet to the tent of Jael the wife of Heber the Kenite (Ethiopian): for there was peace between Jabin the king of Hazor and the house of Heber the Kenite. And Jael went out to meet Sisera, and said unto him, Turn in, my lord, turn in to me; fear not. And when he had turned in unto her into the tent, she covered him with a mantle" (Judges 4:18).

Here a black woman named Jael, identified as the wife of Heber the Kenite several times in Scripture is about to fulfill the prophecy of Deborah. The Kenites (Ethiopians) were respected and even feared by the inhabitants of Canaan. That is one of the reasons that Moses asked their ancestor, Jethro (Hobab), his father in law to go with them into the wilderness to be scouts. Israel, during their exodus from Egypt, had no armies or soldiers or fighting men. These Ethiopians or Kenites were known as warriors that dwelt in the wilderness and they had the respect and fear of the inhabitants of the land. Israel did not have to fight with some of the Canaanites in their journey just because these Kenites were with him. It was Moses' great wisdom to form an alliance with this respected tribe of people as Israel was just coming out of bondage and developing as a nation and people. All they had going for them at that time was the covenant that the Lord had given them. Moses then shared the promises of that covenant with the Kenites, and they were joined as a people (See Numbers 10:29–33).

This respect that the Kenites (Ethiopians) had with the Canaanites is seen by Sisera's willingness to accept Jael's invitation to hide him and protect him from those who were pursuing him. She covered him with a rug or blanket. He had been running, so he was thirsty and asked for water. However, she gave him milk instead. After having run for his life he was likely to be very tired, and giving him milk instead of water would help him to sleep quickly. Sisera asked Jael to watch out for him, and protect him from anyone inquiring if he was there and if one did inquire if a man was there, to say no. When Sisera fell asleep, Jael was used by God to fulfill the prophecy that was spoken by the prophetess Deborah.

> "Then Jael Heber's wife took a nail (tent pin) of the tent, and took an hammer in her hand, and went softly unto him (Sisera), and smote the nail into his temples, and fastened it into the ground: for he was fast asleep and weary. So he died. And, behold, as Barak pursued Sisera, Jael came out to meet him, and said unto him, come, and I will shew thee the man whom thou seekest. And when he came into her tent, behold, Sisera lay dead, and the nail was in his temples. So God subdued on that day Jabin the king of Canaan before the children of Israel" (Judges 4:21–23).

Jael, the wife of Heber the Kenite and a black woman, fulfilled the prophecy that was spoken by Deborah, the prophetess. The honor spoken of by the Lord for the victory in delivering Sisera by the hand of a woman came by Jael. In most modern day preaching of the word, and in the commentaries written by supposedly learned men, Jael is not given any credit or praise for her role in the history of Israel. To these learned men, this black life didn't matter. However, to God this black life did matter and the prophetess Deborah who spoke of her victorious feat gave her praise in the Song of

Deborah. She spoke of herself and Barak, but she said of this black woman named Jael:

> "Blessed **above** women shall Jael the wife of Heber the Kenite be, blessed shall she be above women in the tent. He asked water, and she gave him milk; she brought forth butter in a lordly dish. She put her hand to the nail, and her right hand to the workmen's hammer; and with the hammer she smote Sisera, she smote off his head, when she had pierced and stricken through his temples. At **her** feet he bowed, he fell, he lay down; at **her** feet he bowed, he fell: where he bowed, there he fell down dead" (Judges 5:24–27).

Again, in Scripture, black people are used as a standard of judgment and a standard of God's ways. This black woman, Jael, was even used as a standard in warfare. May the truth of this black woman's important role in Scripture be taught in pulpits and classrooms all over the world. Hopefully, this will happen, especially where people of color need a sense of identity and self-worth. With people of color making up 90% of the world, may the Bible taught truthfully be a main source of that identity and self-worth in seeing characters like Jael as a standard of God's ways and as evidence that blacks lives do matter to God.

This lesson in history is completely contrary to the negative way the Scripture has been used by many in religion and education to portray black people as docile and stupid. The Scriptures have also been used by preachers, even today, to cause people to be subject to sometimes evil or ungodly authority.

Even in education, until recently, the only required reading of anything with black characters beside the European presentation of history was "To Kill a Mockingbird" and "Huckleberry Finn," both portraying black people as stupid and docile.

This positive portrayal of a black woman in Scripture helps us to understand even more so the heroic acts of women like Sojourner Truth and Harriet Tubman, as well as some of the more modern heroes like Shirley Chisolm, the first black candidate for President, or Barbara Jordan, the distinguished Congresswoman from Texas, or Carol Moseley-Braun, the first black female to serve as a United States Senator.

These are just a few of the many black women heroines, many who are not well known, but function in effective leadership roles among the grassroots of people, and especially the grassroots of motherhood in the black community where, in 70% of households, men are missing in action.

May this lesson in Biblical history help to accentuate the great plethora of black women who have added to the betterment of humankind.

---

1 Strong, James H. *Strong's Exhaustive Concordance.*
2 Lockyer, Herbert. *All the Men of the Bible,* p. 40.
3 Johnson, John L. *The Black Biblical Heritage,* p. 135.
4 Lockyer, Herbert. *All the Men of the Bible,* p. 312.
5 Whiston, William. *The Life and Work of Flavius Josephus,* p. 261.
6 Strong, James H. *Strong's Exhaustive Concordance.*
7 Jamieson, Robert, A.R. Fausset, and David Brown. *A Commentary on the Old and New Testaments,* Grand Rapids.
8 Clarke, Adam. *Adam Clark Commentary, Electronic Database.*

CHAPTER 5

Black Characters Who Became "Eyes" for God's People (And God's Purposes)

A Black Harlot Who Became Royal

Rahab – her name means proud; roomy, in any (or every) direction, literally or figuratively. Some English words transliterated from the Hebrew word are, broad, large, at liberty, proud, wide. The Hebrew word comes from a primitive root word meaning to broaden, literally or figuratively. English transliterated words are (be an en- make) large (-ing), make room, make (open) wide.[1] The first part of Rahab's name was the name of an Egyptian god named "Ra." Rahab was an Amorite and belonged to an idolatrous people. Her name also meant **insolence, fierceness**, or **broad** and **spacious**.[2]

As an Amorite, she came from the lineage of Canaan, the son of Ham, whose name means dark or swarthy, black or warm. Rahab was a black woman referred to in Scripture as a harlot. The Scripture says that Joshua sent out two men to secretly spy the land, even specifically, the city of Jericho. Joshua was the captain of the armies of Israel. The spies went out and came to this harlot's house named

Rahab and lodged there. "Rahab's house was built against the town wall with the roof almost level with the ramparts, and with a stairway leading up to a flat roof that appears to be a continuation of the wall. Thus, the people of Jericho knew all about the men who entered and left such a disreputable house."³

It was told by the king of Jericho that men had come by night of the children of Israel to search out the land. The king of Jericho then sent to Rahab, saying, "…Bring forth the men that are come to thee, which are entered into thine house: for they be come to search out all the country" (Joshua 2:3). Rahab took the two men and hid them and said to the king that there came men to her, but I don't know where they are. She said at the time of the shutting of the gate when it was dark, that the men went out and she didn't know in which direction they went. Then to throw them off, she said, pursue after them quickly because you might be able to catch up with them.

> "But she had brought them up to the roof of the house, and hid them with the stalks of flax, which she had laid in order upon the roof. And the men pursued after them the way to Jordan unto the fords; and as soon as they which went after them were gone out, they shut the gate" (Joshua 2:6, 7).

Before the men had laid down on the roof, Rahab told the men that she knew that the Lord had given them the land and that the people are already afraid of Israel, and all the inhabitants of the land were faint or weak because of Israel.

> "For we have heard how the Lord dried up the water of the Red Sea for you, when ye came out of Egypt; and what ye did unto the two kings of the Amorites, that were on the other side of Jordan, Sihon and Og whom ye utterly destroyed. And as soon as we

had heard these things, our hearts did melt, neither did there remain any more courage in any man, because of you; for the Lord your God, he is God in heaven above, and in earth beneath" (Joshua 2:10, 11).

Rahab then made a deal with the two spies and had them to swear to her by the Lord, that since she had shown them kindness, that they would also show kindness to her father's house, and give her a true token that they would save alive her father, mother, brethren, sisters and all that they have, and deliver all their lives from death. "And the men answered her, Our life for yours, if ye utter not this our business. And it shall be, when the Lord hath given us the land, that we will deal kindly and truly with thee" (Joshua 2:14).

Rahab then let the two spies down by a cord through a window because her house was upon the town wall, and she told them to go to the mountain and wait three days until those who pursue you return, then go your way. The spies swore an oath to her and said to bind this scarlet cord in the window that you let us down by, and when we come back into the land, bring all your family into your house and they shall be saved as long as they stay in the house. Then they told her if she uttered their business to anyone, then they are released from the oath. "And she said, According unto your words, so be it. And she sent them away, and they departed: and she bound the scarlet line in the window" (Joshua 2:21).

This black woman, referred to as Rahab the harlot, identified with the people of God, and came under their salvation, despite being a gentile, and changed her and her family's whole course of life. Even though she was a harlot, she was concerned about her family and included them in the oath that she made with the two spies. These men were sent to spy out the land for forty days, but they never left the harlot's house because she assured them that the land was theirs.

Joshua, after a few days, led the army of Israel into Jericho, "And they utterly destroyed all that was in the city, both man and woman, young and old, and ox, and sheep, and ass, with the edge of the sword" (Joshua 6:21). Joshua then honored the oath that the two spies made with Rahab the harlot. He made sure that his first order of business when the walls of Jericho fell was to go in and save Rahab and her house.

> "But Joshua had said unto the two men that had spied out the country, Go into the harlot's house and bring out thence the woman, and all that she hath, as ye sware unto her. And the young men that were spies went in, and brought out Rahab, and her father, and her mother, and her brethren, and all that she had; and they brought out all her kindred, and left them without the camp of Israel" (Joshua 6:22, 23).

Then after Joshua burnt the city with fire and everything that was in it, except the silver, and the gold, and the vessels of brass and iron that were put into the treasury of the house of the Lord, he made sure that Rahab and her family became part of the commonwealth of Israel. "And Joshua saved Rahab the harlot alive, and her father's household, and all that she had; and she dwelleth in Israel even unto this day; because she hid the messengers, which Joshua sent to spy out Jericho" (Joshua 6:25). Though Rahab now had all the privileges and entered in all the covenants that God had given Israel, this black woman became an even more important figure in the history of Israel.

One of the two spies that Rahab sheltered was named Salmon. Salmon was a prince of the house of Judah. Salmon married Rahab, who was a past heathen harlot. She married into one of the leading families of Israel and became an ancestress of our Lord.[4]

In the royal genealogy of Jesus, Rahab is referred to as the wife of Salmon, one of the two spies she sheltered. In turn, she became the mother of Boaz, who married Ruth from whose son, Obed, came Jesse the father of David, through whose line Jesus was born.[5] "Salmon begat Boaz of Rahab" (Matthew 1:5 ASV).

Here again, a black woman became the eyes for Israel in one of their first victories in the land of Canaan. I stated earlier the spies were to search out the land for forty days but never left this harlot's house. She knew all the business of Jericho because most of it passed through her doors. She knew the mindset and attitude of her people and foresaw that they would be defeated and that the Lord was with Israel. So she was not just a harlot, but saw prophetically the will of God, or at least perceived it. The spies needed no other confirmation. They trusted her eyes and her judgment, and so did Joshua.

Here, a black woman, a gentile, referred to as a harlot, identified with God's purposes and God's people, ends up in the lineage of Jesus Christ our Lord! This black woman Rahab was "eyes" for God's people and God's purposes! She fulfilled the reality of "it's not how you start, but how you finish that is important." This black harlot identified and joined with the people of God and ultimately became a part of the royal lineage that birthed Christ Jesus our Lord.

A Black Slave Who Became Noble

Ebed-melech, the Ethiopian eunuch – His name means servant of a king.[6] His name also means slave of the king.[7] He was an Ethiopian eunuch of the palace in King Zedekiah's time who assisted the Prophet Jeremiah in his release from prison.

Black Characters Who Became "Eyes" for God's People

"Now when Ebed-melech the Ethiopian, one of the eunuchs which was in the king's house, heard that they had put Jeremiah in the dungeon; the king then sitting in the gate of Benjamin; Ebed-melech went forth out of the king's house, and spake to the king, saying, My lord the king, these men have done evil in all that they have done to Jeremiah the prophet, whom they have cast into the dungeon; and he is like to die for hunger in the place where he is: for there is no more bread in the city" (Jeremiah 38:7–9).

Previously Jeremiah had prophesied that Jerusalem was going to be given into the hand of the king of Babylon's army, and if you wanted to live, you needed to go now and surrender to the Chaldeans. The Princes of Jerusalem at first thought that Jeremiah was trying to go to the Chaldeans who were broken up from invading Jerusalem for fear of Pharaoh's army. Pharaoh's army had initially come to help Jerusalem against the Chaldeans. But Jeremiah prophesied that Pharaoh's army would not help the king of Judah and would go back to Egypt and that the Chaldean's would come again and fight against Jerusalem and take it and burn it up with fire.

The princes of Judah didn't like Jeremiah's words, and they put him in the dungeon in the house of Jonathan the scribe. However, King Zedekiah sent, and took him out and asked him secretly in his house, "Is there any word from the Lord?" "And Jeremiah said, there is: for, said he, thou shalt be delivered into the hand of the king of Babylon" (Jeremiah 37:17).

Jeremiah then said, "What have I done to offend you? I only gave you the words that the Lord gave me as I have done in the past." Then Jeremiah asked the king to please don't send him back to the house of Jonathan the scribe, lest he died there. "Then Zedekiah the king commanded that they should commit Jeremiah into the court of the prison, and that they should give him daily a piece of bread out of the bakers' street, until all the bread in the city were spent. Thus Jeremiah remained in the court of the prison" (Jeremiah 37:21).

However, when the princes of Jerusalem heard the words that Jeremiah spoke to the people, even in the king's court telling them to go to the Chaldeans so they could live, and that the city would be taken by the hand of the king of Babylon's army, they were infuriated.

> "Therefore the princes said unto the king, We beseech thee, let this man be put to death: for thus he weakeneth the hands of the men of war that remain in this city, and the hands of all the people, in speaking such words unto them: for this man seeketh not the welfare of this people, but the hurt. Then Zedekiah the king said, Behold, he is in your hand: for the king is not he that can do any thing against you. Then took they Jeremiah and cast him into the dungeon of Malchiah the son of Hamme-lech, that was in the court of the prison: and they let down Jeremiah with cords. And in the dungeon there was no water, but mire: so Jeremiah sunk in the mire" (Jeremiah 38:4–6).

For Ebed-melech to go before the king without being bidden was taking his life into his own hands. If you go before the king and he has not bidden you and he is displeased with your presence the custom is that you are killed or imprisoned. Ebed-melech was concerned about the word to the nations more than the people of the nation were. His desire was to free the prophet and the prophetic word that was needed to keep the nation in the way of the Lord. After Ebed-melech made his life-threatening appeal for the life of Jeremiah to Zedekiah the king, he gave him permission to rescue Jeremiah.

> "Then the king commanded Ebed-melech the Ethiopian, saying, Take from hence thirty men with thee, and take up Jeremiah the

prophet out of the dungeon, before he die. So Ebed-melech took the men with him, and went into the house of the king under the treasury, and took thence old cast clouts and old rotten rags, and let them down by cords into the dungeon to Jeremiah. And Ebed-melech the Ethiopian said unto Jeremiah, Put now these old cast clouts and rotten rags under thine armholes under the cords. And Jeremiah did so. So they drew up Jeremiah with cords and took him up out of the dungeon: and Jeremiah remained in the court of the prison" (Jeremiah 38:10–13).

Even as a slave, Ebed-melech was a credit to his class, as well a credit to the class of people, Israel, which enslaved him. "It is said of Ebed-melech that he was an Ethiopian which means that he was a heathen and of despicable type at that time."[8] "Can the Ethiopian change his skin?" Can we change our skin as black people in the United States? Can we change the attitude of racism that exists in our society? Can we change our history? No! But we can change our future and set a course for our destiny.

We can't change the racism that exists in our society – But we don't have to be bound to it in our mind, our attitude, and in our spirit. There are some negatives we can shed off for the Kingdom's sake. "…We must through much tribulation (trouble, pressure) enter into the kingdom of God" (Acts 14:22). There are also some attributes that we can add for the Kingdom's sake. "Can the Ethiopian change his skin?"

"No! But this Ethiopian had a transformed moral character and was a triumph of grace in the clan to which he belonged. The Eastern eunuchs were a pitilessly cruel race, whose delight was to wound and vex. No clan had a worse reputation for cruelty."[9] Remember that the Ethiopians were historically a warrior nation and were feared by the inhabitants of the land. They were the third nation in the Egyptian Empire and had kings that were Pharaohs during the Egyptian dynasty. That is one of the reasons that Moses asked the Kenites, a faction of the Ethiopians to be scouts for Israel in the wilderness because they knew the way, and they could be for them instead of eyes or eyes in the wilderness. Now, as warriors, under captivity, they had been reduced down to slaves, and not just regular slaves, but eunuch slaves. Of course they would be an angry and cruel clan.

"But here again Ebed-melech was different. He was as kind as the rest of his clan was cruel. Kitto calls him, "The benevolent Eunuch." Then he is likewise described **as a servant of the king**. Royal servants were usually a godless company. But Ebed-melech was as faithful a servant to God as he was to king Zedekiah. He loved the prophet Jeremiah and risked his own life to save the man of God."[10]

Among the lesson to be gleaned from the record of this eunuch who was greater than his fellows are:

1) He was superior to his surroundings.[11] He did not become a prisoner to his surroundings or circumstances. Just like Joseph, who got better, not bitter when he was in prison. Or like Moses, a prince in Egypt and then had to flee to Midian which means brawling, discord, strife. Or David who had to flee to the wilderness, because of King Saul, and could have become a heathen, wild, and animal-like. Or Jeremiah, who was put in prison. All these men were processed by their surroundings, not destroyed.

2) He was not limited or bound to his cultural, racial, educational, traditional, physical, environmental or economic status. "As a man thinketh in his heart, so is he." Having a vision of God frees us from the present.

3) "He put more pretentious people to shame (See Romans 11:11; Acts 13:46).

4) He had the courage to put action to his convictions"[12] (See James 1:22 -25)
5) He was able to adjust and relate to a different class and race of people (of importance) for God's sake – 1 Corinthians 9:19, 22, 23 – even in suffering – Philippians 1:27–30 – Acts 9:15, 16. A man's gift makes room for him, but there's a processing of character to conform to the anointing of the gift.
6) He could handle authority over other people (Jeremiah 38:10). He was given 30 men (a type of ransom of men), even though he was a slave (See Luke 19:16, 17; Luke 16:10–12).
7) "He achieved a great service with poor instruments. Old rags and cords! God can use weak things for the accomplishment of His plan – 1 Corinthians 1:26–29.
8) His faith and trust in God were the secret of his noble life"[13] – Proverbs 3:5–8; Psalm 37:3. He trusted in the Lord and did good, and he was preserved in the land.
9) "He was divinely rewarded. God is a grand Paymaster."[14]

"Now the word of the Lord came unto Jeremiah, while he was shut up in the court of the prison, saying, go and speak to Ebed-melech the Ethiopian, saying, Thus said the Lord of hosts, the God of Israel; Behold, I will bring my words upon this city for evil, and not for good; and they shall be accomplished in that day before thee. But I will deliver thee in that day, saith the Lord; and thou shalt not be given into the hand of the men of whom thou art afraid. For I will surely deliver thee, and thou shalt not fall by the sword, but thy life shall be for a **prey** unto thee: because thou hast put thy trust in me, saith the Lord.

The word prey means "booty or spoil. It means a gift or spoil of purpose.[15] This black man, Ebed-melech referred to as an Ethiopian eunuch, was given by the Lord as a gift of purpose to Jeremiah the prophet and Judah. God personally declared his deliverance from the captors because of his trust in God. This Ethiopian eunuch knew the Lord more than many that were in Judah, and guided them in the way of the Lord in delivering, preserving and believing the prophetic word through the mouth of Jeremiah the prophet. Part of God's covenant with Abraham was that he would give certain people to Abraham, not just to defeat, but as gifts to his people Israel. "In the same day the Lord made a covenant with Abram, saying, Unto thy seed have I given this land, from the river of Egypt unto the great river, the river Euphrates: The Kenites, and the Kenizzites, and the Kadmonites..." (Genesis 15:18, 19). These are all black people and black lands. Ebed-melech the Ethiopian (Kenite) is one of the covenant gifts given by God to Israel to help "see" their way out of the mire of judgment and defeat, and to release again the prophetic word to the nation. As we find our God-given purpose and line up with our destiny, may the black segment of the church be received as unique gifts to the Body of Christ and the nations (Psalm 72:10).

A Black Man Who Shared Christ's Burden

Simon of Cyrene – "A Cyrenian (Lybian) who was compelled to bear the cross after Jesus."[16] "And as they led him away, they laid hold upon one Simon, a Cyrenian, coming out of the country, and on him they laid the cross, that he might bear it after Jesus" (Luke 23:26).

"The dramatic history in this verse does not come through. In reality, black Simon the Cyrenian just did not happen by the day of the crucifixion. He was part of a vibrant movement. It was as important that he was there as it was also for his son, Alexander. Mark 15:21 identifies Simon as "The father of Alexander and Rufus."[17] "Alexander and Rufus were well-known members of the church at [probably] Rome." (See Acts 19:33; Romans 16:13).[18] Simon and his family were known to Mark. Mark was well informed about Simon and his sons. It is evident that he knew Simon's personal life history. "Alexander, a strong and effective preacher of the gospel, was also there. So were hundreds of other followers of this movement. So Simon did not stroll over to the crowd out of sheer curiosity to see what all of the excitement was about."[19]

"Today's movies have missed a significant fact when depicting this highly emotional, historical day in Jerusalem. There are no Blacks to be seen. The stern-faced, heavily armed soldiers are there. Curious and weeping spectators are there. Therefore the movie would have us believe there were no Blacks involved in the struggle to support Jesus of Nazareth. Yet there are letters chiseled in concrete over a door in Jerusalem. It says 'Here Simon the Cyrenian helped Jesus carry the cross.' In one of the Hollywood religious spectaculars, a Roman soldier ordered Simon to help Jesus, but the Simon in the movie was white."[20]

"The fact that Simon traveled from the black land of Cyrene to be with Jesus on this day explains the presence of a dynamic movement. Historically the day of the Crucifixion was the turning point in a great and growing popular movement, which we now call Christianity. The execution of Jesus of Nazareth by the Romans was simply a powerful stimulation for the growth of this movement later called Christianity."[21]

"To add credence to Black participation in this movement, obvious facts point the way. Blacks were a substantial part of the population in Palestine. They were part of the Jesus movement from the beginning. Blacks had been present in Jerusalem throughout its stormy history. Central Africans had been familiar with the one-God concept for thousands of years. The early Black Egyptians knew about it. St. Augustine gave them credit for this in his Fourth Century writings."[22] That was one of the good things that St. Augustine wrote in relation to black people.

"Blacks were among the throngs who had heard Jesus speak. They followed Him to Jerusalem. They walked with Him as everyone else did. They touched Him."[23] "Simon the Cyrenian was at this time, a black farmer living outside of ancient Jerusalem."[24] "Simon was originally from Cyrenia in present day Libya in North Africa.[25] Simon was a descendant of Phut, who was the son of Ham (See Genesis 10:6). Remember that Hams name means dark or swarthy, black and warm.

"Simon walked in the footsteps of Jesus, bearing His cross. He saw Jesus nailed to the cross. Simon saw Jesus hanging on the cross. Simon experienced the crucifixion or at least the sufferings of Jesus. He saw the blood of Jesus"[26] and probably touched it.

"Roman Catholics believe that Simon was killed by the sword on the Isle of Chios in the First Century. Chios is an island in the Aegean Sea off the West Coast of Asia Minor."[27]

At Jesus' most devastating time in His earthly walk; when He was in the way of the road to Golgotha to complete our redemption, He could not physically continue the burden of bearing the cross by Himself. Of all people, entrance stage-left, there came a black man to help Him and keep Him in the way of Calvary. Jesus probably had blood caked around His eyes and couldn't see clearly. But this black man became eyes for Jesus to help Him stay in the way of the

Cross, though humanly it was hard to bear. A black man helped our Lord Jesus Christ carry the cross. And so we have identified and bore most of the burdens of society in history. But may we in this day and time, experience the other side of the cross, and share in Christ's resurrection power and manifested redemption and blessings. "The first shall be last," but the prophecy concludes "The last shall be first!"

1. Strong, James H. *Strong's Exhaustive Concordance.*
2. Lockyer, Herbert. *All the Women of the Bible*, p. 130.
3. *Ibid.*, p. 131.
4. *Ibid.*
5. *Ibid.*, p. 130, 131.
6. Strong, James H. *Strong's Exhaustive Concordance.*
7. Lockyer, Herbert. *All the Men of the Bible*, p. 94.
8. *Ibid.*
9. *Ibid.*
10. *Ibid.*
11. *Ibid.*
12. *Ibid.*
13. *Ibid.*
14. *Ibid.*
15. Strong, James H. *Strong's Exhaustive Concordance.*
16. Loycker, Herbert. *All the Men of the Bible*, p. 317.
17. Hyman, Mark. *Blacks Who Died for Jesus*, p. 1.
18. Orr, James. *The International Standard Bible Encyclopedia, Volume IV*, p. 2795.
19. Hyman, Mark. *Blacks Who Died for Jesus*, p. 1.
20. *Ibid.*
21. *Ibid.* p. 3.
22. *Ibid.*
23. *Ibid.*
24. The Kansas City Call Newspaper. *Two Blacks Helped Make Today's Easter.*
25. *Ibid.*
26. Rhoades, F. S. *Black Characters and References of the Holy Bible*, p. 76.
27. Hyman, Mark. *Blacks Who Died for Jesus*, p. 3.

PART II

Introduction

Preaching, teaching and talking about black people in the Bible is still a strange and unique thing even in the 21st Century. Even in Christian and Evangelical circles this is still a strange phenomenon. It is because of the purposeful directing of history and society to give honor to and exalt the people who are in power. Usually, history is told from a perspective of lies to benefit the people who are in power, that is, what is referred to as official history, depending on the country who is doing the officiating. In the Western Hemisphere, the white race has mostly been in power for the last 500 years and has succeeded in developing a system of oppression that affects 80 to 90% of the rest of the world.

That oppression reaches down to education, society, and even religion or Christianity. That is that every effort must be made to present a positive picture of the race in power (the white race) and in turn, a negative picture of any other race, especially if exalting another race would cast a bad shadow on the white race. This is understandable in society because it has been done for hundreds of years in many countries. However, the line should be drawn when it comes to Christianity which is a spiritual movement based on **truth**. The founder of our Christian movement Jesus Christ is called, "The Way, the **Truth**, and the Life." The Administrative Agent of our Christian movement is called the Holy Spirit, Who is the Spirit of **Truth**. The element for building and developing this Christian movement is called the Word of **Truth**.

Truth is so important that when Jesus Christ our Lord was pressed by the power structure of the world, that was evidenced by Pontius Pilate, the representative of the Roman Empire at that time, as to why He was here, and why He was upsetting the religious power structure of that time, that was evidenced by the chief priests and scribes of that day, He answered: "…To this end was I born, and for this cause came I into the world, that I should **bear witness unto the truth**. Every one that is of the **truth** heareth my voice" (John 18:37).

Then Jesus responded to that same religious power structure evidenced by the scribes and Pharisees, who had a hard time accepting Who He was, because He did not come from their order, by saying, "And ye shall know the **truth**, and the **truth** shall make you free" (John 8:32).

Hopefully, the church and our religious institutions have matured enough to fulfill our role as being "the pillar and ground of **truth**" and accept the truth of the presence of many black characters in the Bible which is commensurate with the 80 to 90% of the world that are people of color. The second part of this book is written with this commission of truth in mind.

As in part one of this book, most of the references in this book will come from my research and study of the Scriptures since the Bible is the main reference to my presentation of characters. Other references will come mostly from Bible helps and commentaries that substantiate or witness to my research from the Scriptures.

CHAPTER 6

There Was Always a Mixed Multitude with Israel

"And the children of Israel journeyed from Rameses to Succoth, about six hundred thousand on foot that were men, beside children. And a mixed multitude went up also with them; and flocks, and herds, even very much cattle" (Exodus 12:37, 38).

It is important to know that there were many other nations that were with Israel when they left Egypt and started their journey in the wilderness. There were Ethiopians or Cushites, also referred to as Kenites. There were Canaanites, Amorites, Hittites, Egyptians and others of the lineage of Ham that were part of that "...mixed multitude..." The Hebrew word for "**mixed** means the **web (or transverse threads of cloth)**; also a **mixture, (or mongrel race)**. Some other English words that are transliterated from this Hebrew word are Arabia, mingled people, mixed (multitude), woof. This Hebrew word comes from a primitive root word that means **to braid**, that is, **intermix; technically, to traffic (as if by barter); also or give to be security (as a kind of exchange)**. Other English words that are transliterated from this primitive root word are en-gage, (inter-) meddle (with), mingle (self), mortgage, occupy, give pledges, be (-come, put in) surely, undertake."[1] The margin of the Kings James Version of this Hebrew word reads "**Including others beside Israelites.**"[2]

We understand from the use of this word and its definition that this mixed multitude was not just some people going along for the ride, but people from other nations that were involved with Israel in very personal ways. Either through inter-marriage or as the definition suggest, "to traffic (as if by barter). Barter means to trade by exchange of commodities rather than by the use of money.[3] Some of the people of other nations were given to Israel as an exchange for some service or because of some covenant or league. Some were through covenant inclusion given in exchange for security, like the Kenites (Ethiopians) (See Numbers 10:29–33). Some like Rahab, an Amorite, and her family recognized the hand of God with the children of Israel and came in league with them or made covenant with them.

It is important also to know that there were proselytes of other nations among Israel. Even the law provided for "...strangers in your midst..." concerning the Passover provision.

> "And the Lord said unto Moses and Aaron, This is the ordinance of the Passover: There shall no stranger eat thereof: But every man's servant that is bought for money, when thou hast circumcised him, then shall he eat thereof. A foreigner and an hired servant shall not eat thereof. In one house shall it be eaten; thou shalt not carry forth ought of the flesh abroad out of the house; neither shall ye break a bone thereof. All the congregation of Israel shall keep it. And when a stranger shall sojourn with thee, and will keep the Passover to the Lord, let all his males be circumcised, and then let him come near and keep it; and he shall be as one that is born in the land: for no uncircumcised person shall eat thereof.

One law shall be to him that is homeborn, and unto the stranger that sojourneth among you" (Exodus 12:43–49).

God gave specific instruction on how to treat a stranger in the midst of Israel, but there were many people that came to Israel and witnessed the hand of God and eventually joined themselves to Israel or became friends of Israel. Many just came among them and respected them as a people. "Also thou shalt not oppress a stranger: for ye know the heart of a stranger, seeing ye were strangers in the land of Egypt" (Exodus 23:9).

God also gave specific instructions to Israel on how to harvest their crops and their fields in relation to strangers and the poor. Through giving this kind of instructions, He made provision for strangers in Israel. God knew that many other nations and people groups would join God's chosen people as a part of His purposes.

> "And when ye reap the harvest of your land thou shalt not wholly reap the corners of thy field, neither shalt thou gather the gleanings of thy harvest. And thou shalt not glean thy vineyard, neither shalt thou gather every grape of thy vineyard; thou shalt leave them for the poor and stranger: I am the Lord your God" (Leviticus 19:9, 10).

Then the Lord went further and instructed Israel not to do anything to "vex" or oppress the strangers that travel with you in your land. Don't do to them what was done to you as strangers in another land. Here the Lord established civil rights for strangers who elected to travel with Israel, be in Israel or just be among the Israelites, seeing you are eventually to be a witness to other nations, and other nations are to be blessed through you.

> "And if a stranger sojourn with thee in your land, ye shall not vex him. But the stranger that dwelleth with you shall be unto you

as one born among you, and thou shalt love him as thyself: for ye were strangers in the land of Egypt: I am the Lord your God" (Leviticus 19:33, 34).

God knew that His covenant to Abraham had provisions for all nations and that as Israel continued in obedience to God's will, they would be the instrument to take those provisions and blessings to all nations. Therefore, all nations would eventually be a part of the redemptive plan of God that He started, and that had its roots in the initial promises to Abraham, that later became covenants when Abraham began to believe God and cut covenant with Him (See also Leviticus 23:22; Leviticus 24:22, Genesis 15:1-21).

We will see later that a priest and people that were a part of other nations and ethnic groups introduced Abram to God. People of other nations and ethnic groups led Moses and his elders in their first worship sacrifice to the Lord. And they helped Israel learn to build altars and worship God. This is because these people already knew the Most High God and had a One-God concept before Israel even became a nation. There was no travel ban or barring of people from other nations by God.

---

1 Strong, James H. *Strong's Exhaustive Concordance.*
2 *King James Version of the Bible (The).* Thomas Nelson Publishers.
3 *Dictionary.com Unabridged.* Based on the Random House Dictionary, Random House, Inc: 2011.

CHAPTER 7

Black Priests in the Bible

Melchizedek

Melchizedek – Is first introduced in Scripture as the king of Salem. "His name means **king of right**. This Hebrew definition comes from two words which mean **a king, royal, to reign** or **to ascend the throne**; and another Hebrew word that means **the right**, nationally, morally, or legally; also **equity** or figuratively **prosperity**. Some of the English transliterations of the word means even or that which altogether just (-ice), or right (-eous)."[1] "He is also identified as the king of righteousness or justice. Herbert Lockyer refers to him as the priest and king of Salem, who met Abraham and blessed him."[2] However, the King James Bible refers to him still as Melchizedek, and not only the king of Salem but the **priest of the most high God**, not the priest of Salem. Salem means peaceful, complete or friendly. (Strong's Exhaustive Concordance.)

"Although a mysterious figure, Melchizedek is yet a figure of great importance. His biography is short. He comes before us in history (Genesis 14); in prophecy (Psalm 110); in doctrine (Hebrews

7), and prefigures Christ's priesthood. He is King of Righteousness, and King of Peace."³

Since Melchizedek was the King of Salem, which is the ancient city of Jerusalem before it was inhabited by Israel, Melchizedek was a black man of the lineage of Ham, through Canaan. Remember that Ham means dark or swarthy, black or warm. The controversy of his background is because the Scripture says, concerning Melchizedek, "To whom also Abraham gave a tenth part of all; first being by interpretation King of righteousness, and after that also King of Salem, which is, King of peace; without father, without mother, without descent, having neither beginning of days, nor end of life; but made like unto the Son of God; abideth a priest continually" (Hebrews 7:2, 3).

However, Melchizedek was an actual person in history from the account in Genesis 14:18–20, and in history. The controversy about who he really is because of the scripture that says, "…without father, without mother, without descent, having neither beginning of days, nor end of life…" This, of course, would be a problem from a Jewish perspective, where who begot who, and who married who, and who their children were, and how they lived, and when they died is recorded for thousands of years. But there is no such record for Melchisedec! **That is because he is no Jew!** He is of the lineage of Ham, and would not necessarily be listed in the Chronicles of Israel.

He is the King of Salem which is ancient Jeru-salem. The Prophet Ezekiel gives us the roots and history of ancient Jerusalem. "Son of man, cause Jerusalem to know her abominations, And say, Thus saith the Lord God unto Jerusalem; Thy birth and thy nativity is of the land of Canaan; thy father was an Amorite, and thy mother an Hittite" (Ezekiel 16:2, 3). In other words, your daddy was black and your mama was black. These are black people who were descendants of Ham through the lineage of Canaan, which was the land that was promised to Israel for an inheritance through Abraham. Therefore, Melchisedec would have to be either an Amorite or a Hittite as king of Salem. This black man's lineage traces back to Ham.

"The relation between Melchizedek and Christ as type and antitype is made in the Epistle to the Hebrews to consist in the following particulars: each was a priest (1) who is not of the Levitical tribe; (2) who is superior to Abraham; (3) whose beginning and end are unknown; (4) who is not only a priest but also a king of righteousness and peace. "Without father," etc. (Hebrews 7:3), refers to priestly genealogies. Melchizedek is not found on the register of the only line of legitimate priests; his father's name is not recorded, nor his mother's; no evidence points out his line of descent from Aaron. **It is not affirmed that he had no father or that he was not born at any time or died on any day**, but these facts were found nowhere on the register of the Leviticial priesthood."[4]

"What is the meaning of "without father, without mother, without genealogy, having neither beginning of days nor end of life"? **Not that it was actually so, but that it appeared so in the Old Testament Records.** Levitical Priests were Priests because of their genealogy. But Melchizedek, without genealogy, was the recognized Priest"[5] of the Most High God, a black king/priest in the Bible.

Jesus in His priestly function declared that He came after the "order" of the Melchisedek Priesthood. "Order" means the style or fashion of the Melchizedek priesthood or order.

Jesus liked this black man's fashion or style. His style or priesthood was before there was a Levitical or Aaronic Priesthood for Israel. This black priest had a style that Jesus our Lord emanated. This black priest stood before God and then stood before the people and represented God to them before there even was a nation of Israel formed, or an Egyptian Empire or a Babylonian Empire.

With the lack of fathers present in the black family and home in the United States, there is a shortage in images of dignity from the male perspective in the black community. However, I have found power in referring to this ancestor as one of the first examples of priesthood dignity or the dignity of those who represent God to a people. Melchisedek was a black symbol of dignity which even Jesus Christ our Lord drew from, and fashioned Himself after his style.

Jethro

Jethro – "His name means **his excellence**; referred to as Moses' father in law. The Hebrew meaning of this name comes from a Hebrew word that **properly means an overhanging**, that is, (by implication) **an excess, superiority, remainde**r; also **a small rope (as hanging free)**. Some English transliterations of this word mean abundant, cord, exceeding, excellency (-ent), what they leave, that hath left, plentifully, remnant, residue, rest, string, with."[6] "His name also means pre-eminence or excellence. He was also called Reuel or Raguel meaning "friend of God" in Exodus 2:18 and Numbers 10:29, and Jethro in Exodus 4:18. He was a priest of Midian."[7]

Jethro, Moses father in law, was also referred to as a Kenite, who is a faction of the Ethiopians that came from the lineage of Ham, by way of Cush his son, whose name means black or Ethiopian. Jethro, also called Reuel, served as the priest or the "King James Bible margin says **chief** of Midian."[8] "The author of the Pentateuch refers to Hobab, the son of Raguel the Midianite, Moses; father in law (Numbers 10:29), but that of the Book of Judges classes him as a "Kenite: Now Heber the Kenite, which was of the children of Hobab the father in law of Moses (Judges 4:11). This seeming discrepancy is reconciled by the fact that the "Kenites" were a Midianitish clan"⁹ as far as where they dwelt. Moses fled from the face of Pharaoh, once it was known that he had slain an Egyptian who he saw smiting a Hebrew, one of his brethren. He fled to the land of Midian and dwelt there. "Now the priest (chief) of Midian had seven daughters; and they came and drew water, and filled the troughs to water their father's flock" (Exodus 2:16). The shepherds came and drove them away, who were woman shepherdess, but Moses stood up for them and helped them and watered their flock.

They went home sooner than they usually did, and their father, Reuel (Jethro) inquired as to why they were home so early. They told him about how the Egyptian had delivered them out of the hand of the shepherds and had also drawn enough water for them to water their flock. Reuel asked his daughters, where the man was, and why did you leave him. He then told them to go and get the man so he could eat bread with them. The Scripture says, "And Moses was content to dwell with the man: and he gave Moses Zipporah his daughter" (Exodus2:21), who later on in Scripture is referred to as Ethiopian or Cushite (See Numbers 12:1).

"Moses kept the flock of Jethro, his father in law, the priest of Midian: and he led the flock to the backside of the desert, and came to the mountain of God, even to Horeb" (Exodus 3:1). Moses dwelt with Jethro his father in law and his daughter Zipporah for 40 years, learning how to be a shepherd. He then had an encounter with God at the mountain of God where this black priest served. It was here that Moses was given his commission as a deliver for the children of Israel from Egypt. (See Exodus 3:1–Exodus 4:17).

Moses was given his commission and call to deliver the children of Israel from Egypt and instructed by God on how to bring the deliverance. He was to bring them forth out of Egypt and then bring them to serve God upon this same mountain where this black man, Jethro had been serving God as a priest.

> "And Moses said unto God, Who am I, that I should go unto Pharaoh, and that I should bring forth the children of Israel out of Egypt? And he said, Certainly I will be with thee; and this shall be a token unto thee, that I have sent thee; When thou hast brought forth the people out of Egypt, ye shall serve God upon this mountain" (Exodus 3:11, 12).

God continued to instruct Moses about His name, and what he should say, and how He would use his rod to do signs and wonders in Egypt because Pharaoh's heart would be hardened and he would not want to release the children of Israel from bondage. After God finished his instruction, Moses then went to this black man, his father in law, the priest serving at the mountain of God in the land of Midian, and asked Jethro's permission to go and deliver the children of Israel.

> "And Moses went and returned to Jethro his father in law, and said unto him, Let me go, I pray thee, and return unto my brethren which are in Egypt, and see whether they be yet alive. And Jethro said to Moses, Go in peace" (Exodus 4:18).

Moses had served this black man for 40 years and had married his daughter Zipporah. He had great respect for him not only as his father in law but also his employer and teacher, as well as his status as chief of his people and the priest of the Most High God serving at the mountain of God.

Once Moses delivered the children of Israel from Egypt with signs and wonders and an exhibition of the mighty hand of God, he brought them back to the mountain of God where He met God, and where this black priest Jethro served.

> "When Jethro, the priest of Midian, Moses' father in law, heard of all that God had done for Moses, and for Israel his people, and that the Lord had brought Israel out of Egypt: Then Jethro, Moses' father in law, took Zipporah, Moses' wife, after he had sent her back, And her two sons...And Jethro, Moses' father in law, came with his sons and his wife unto Moses into the wilderness, where he encamped at the mount of God: And he said unto Moses, I thy father in law Jethro am come unto thee, and thy wife, and her two sons with her" (Exodus 18:1–3a, 5, 6).

After having served Jethro, his father in law for 40 years, Moses was submissive to him and very respectful. After all, this black man had been his teacher and taught him how to be a shepherd, which prepared him eventually to be a deliverer for his people. It is important to see that God was instrumental in this man Jethro's name, to mean excellency. In Exodus 18:1, "for the meaning of the name *Jethro* the margin in the King James Bible says, *that is, Excellency*."[10] In the scriptures, and in the Hebrew culture, a name denotes character and purpose. It is not like the random choice of names that we give to children in today's culture. God wanted Moses to receive an 'impartation by association" of excellency through this black priest, named Jethro. Moses evidently had received this kind of impartation and had a very high regard and respect for Jethro. In fact, his first order of business once he got back to the mountain of God was to rehearse the events of the deliverance with Jethro. "And Moses went out to meet his father in law, and did obeisance, and kissed him; and they asked each other of their welfare; and they came into the tent" (Exodus 18:7).

Moses then rehearsed to his father in law, Jethro, all that the Lord had done to Pharaoh and to Egypt, and all the miracles and struggles, and how the Lord had delivered Israel. Jethro then rejoiced for all the goodness that the Lord had shown to Israel and for His great deliverance of the people from the bondage of Egypt. Then Jethro made a proclamation saying, "Now I know that the Lord is greater than all gods: for in the thing wherein they dealt proudly he was above them" (Exodus 18:11).

Moses recognized the authority and stature of this great man of God, which happened to be his father in law and teacher. Then this black priest did an amazing thing in the history of Israel, but something very common to him. He led Moses, Aaron and all the elders in a burnt-offering and sacrifices for God. This black priest, Jethro, knew about sacrifices and burnt offerings for God even before Moses did. He was a priest of God before the Aaronic priesthood was even set up. Moses probably learned how to sacrifice before the Lord when he was under the leadership of Jethro for 40 years in the land of Midian. "And Jethro, Moses father in law, took a burnt offering and sacrifices for God: and Aaron came, and all the elders of Israel, **to eat bread with Moses's father in law before God**" (Exodus 18:12).

The next day Moses sat to judge the people, and the people came to Moses from the morning until the evening. Jethro, Moses father in law saw this and asked him, what are you doing? Why do you sit here alone and the people stand by you from morning until evening? "And Moses said unto his father in law, Because the people come unto me to inquire of God: When they have a matter, they come unto me, and I judge between one and another, and I do make them know the statutes of God, and his laws" (Exodus 18:15, 16).

From Jethro's counsel to Moses, "the present system of our Courts, which is the plan of their subdivision in inferior, superior and supreme courts, was born in the brain of this black man Jethro. The civilized world is justly proud of this subdivision of its Judiciary system, which secured to man the possibility of justice, according to human standards. This system has evolved in its present comprehensive scope by the Anglo-Saxon race, which leads the world in matters judicial; but, as said above, the genius of that system is the product of the brain of a black man, whose name was Jethro, the father in law of Moses.[11]

> "And Moses' father in law said unto him, the thing that thou doest is not good. Thou wilt surely wear away, both thou, and this people that is with thee; for this thing is too heavy for thee; thou art not able to perform it thyself alone. Hearken now unto my voice, I will give thee counsel, and God shall be with thee: Be thou for the people to Godward, that thou mayest bring the causes unto God: And thou shalt teach them ordinances and laws, and shalt shew them the way wherein they must walk, and the work that they must do. Moreover thou shalt provide out of all the people able men, such as fear God, men of truth, hating covetousness; and place such over them, to be rulers of thousands, and rulers of hundreds, rulers of fifties, and rulers of tens: And let them judge the people at all seasons; and it shall be, that every great matter they shall bring unto thee, but every small matter they shall judge: so shall it be easier for thyself, and they shall bear the burden with thee. If thou shall do this thing, and God command thee so, then thou shalt be able to endure, and all this people shall also go to their place in peace. So Moses hearkened to the voice of his father in law, and did all that he had said" (Exodus 18:17–24).

What a tremendous contribution of wisdom to Moses, his people, and the rest of world came from this black man, Jethro. "The suggestion of Jethro that there should be 'Rulers of Tens,' 'Rulers of Fifties,' Rulers of Hundreds,' and 'Rulers of Thousands' reminds us most forcibly of the hierarchy which remains in the Judicial system of civilized countries at the present time. These 'rulers' were the prototype of the present-day 'Justices' who preside and dispense justice in either 'Municipal,' 'County,' 'Circuit,' or 'Appellate' courts according to the gravity of the cases or the necessity for an appeal against the decision of a lower court.[12]

What a glorious sense of pride should be in the hearts of black people across the world and especially in Christendom when the facts of history are known in wider circles. "It was a black man, Jethro whose creative genius gave to the world the idea of having a Chief Justice. The English nation is justly proud of their Lord High Chancellor; and the citizens of the United States of America, are equally proud of the eminent jurists which comprise the Supreme Court of the United States, presided over by a Chief Justice. But it is nevertheless good to remember the fact that the idea of the necessity of there being a Chief Justice originated in the brain of the black priest Jethro when he suggested that his son in law, Moses should hold that position among the Hebrew children."[13] (See also Numbers 10:29–33; Judges 1:16; Judges 4:11; 1 Samuel 15:6; Numbers 12:1; Habakkuk 3:7).

But even with that pride based on a black man so contributing to the structure of our modern day justice system, there is a deep sense of frustration along with that pride. That frustration is based on the modern day injustices that are perpetrated on black people, especially black youth, in the modern day court systems and proceedings.

God's original intent in establishing judges and using this black priest, named Jethro, to be the originator in developing this system among the Hebrew populous can be understood in Psalm 82.

Here God shares His purpose in establishing judges as part of His ordination. God says that they stand among the magistrates and the mighty judges like standing among the gods. God refers to the magistrates and mighty judges as gods because they have the power of life and death in their mouth just like God does.

In Psalm 82, God is rebuking them because they have lost their purpose in being one of the protectors of the foundations by which the earth was established. In verse 2, God asks them how long will they, the judges, judge unjustly by accepting the person of the wicked or the well to do or the wealthy. The judges back then had begun to favor the rich or the well to do, or the wealthy just like today. You have to just about be rich to hire lawyers to get justice today based on how the justice system has digressed.

In verse 3, God reiterates their original purpose in the earth. "Defend the poor and fatherless: do justice to the afflicted and needy." Verse 4, "Deliver the poor and needy: rid them out of the hand of the wicked." Here God reveals His intent in balancing the justice and morality of the inhabitors of the earth. Judges were established to re-enforce justice for those who are poor, fatherless, afflicted, and needy against those who are wealthy or have means. Those who are wealthy or have means can buy or pay for the finest help to make sure the law favors them or responds to their causes.

The costs of good attorneys to represent your interest are beyond the means of most people who are poor, fatherless, afflicted and needy. Such is the state that our present justice system has degraded to today.

God then concludes in verse 5, "They know not, neither will they understand, they walk on in darkness…" God is referring to the magistrates and the mighty judges who know not the law of God and no longer represent Him.

Because of this God states that all the **foundations** of the earth are **out of course**. From the Hebrew meaning of the word **foundations**, God is saying that which He laid for a foundation or ordained for a foundation to establish the earth is out of course, because these magistrates and mighty judges do not know the Lord or the law of God.

God finishes by saying that I considered you to be like gods even though you are the children of the Most High God. But because of your neglect to know God or the law of God, "…you shall die like men and fall like one of the princes." (See verse 7).

The final verse is the cry that I have today, because the justice system in the United States is the same way for blacks, and the poor, needy, fatherless and afflicted. As black people, we have for hundreds of years gone to the courts for justice and found "just us" being sent to jail with unjust sentences and "just us" being taken advantage of by those who have means or privilege, or those in power. It is "just us" who are being housed and killed and mistreated in our prison systems.

From the lynchings of the past with no implications of justice, to the 70% of the male prison population comprised of black men, to the many police killings and brutality, like Michael Brown in Ferguson, Missouri and Eric Garner in Staten Island, New York. Like Trayvon Martin and Jordan Davis in Florida, Tamar Rice in Cleveland, Ohio and Philando Castile in St. Paul, Minnesota and Sandra Bland in Waller County, Texas and Terrance Cruther in Tulsa, Oklahoma and Keith Scott in Charlotte, North Carolina and Walter Scott in Charleston, South Carolina and Alton Sterling in Baton Rouge, Louisiana or the more than 250 black people killed by police in 2016, to the war on drugs and crime which was really a war on black people. Unfortunately today, it seems many judges do not stand up and defend the poor, the needy, the fatherless and the afflicted, nor value the lives of black and brown people. Like the final verse of Psalm 82, we also cry today, "Arise, O God, judge the earth: for thou shalt inherit all nations." (Psalm 82:8).

1. Strong, James H. *Strong's Exhaustive Concordance.*
2. Lockyer, Herbert. *All the Men of the Bible*, p. 254, 255.
3. *Ibid.*, p. 255.
4. Unger, Merrill F. *The New Unger's Bible Dictionary*, p. 832.
5. Halley, Henry H. *Halley's Bible Handbook*, p. 652.
6. Strong, James H. *Strongs's Exhaustive Concordance.*
7. Lockyer, Herbert. *All the Men of the Bible*, p. 188.
8. *King James Version of the Bible (The).* Thomas Nelson Publishers.
9. Holly, Alonzo Potter. *God and the Negro*, p. 63.
10. *King James Version of the Bible (The).* Thomas Nelson Publishers.
11. Holly, Alonzo Potter. *God and the Negro*, p. 64.
12. *Ibid.*, p. 66.
13. *Ibid.*, p. 67.

CHAPTER 8

Black Leaders in the Bible – Old Testament

Caleb

Caleb – "whose name means *forcible dog*, or *attack dog*."[1] His name also means *bold, impetuous (also an animal name, meaning 'dog')*."[2] "Dog" is a term used for Gentiles by the Jews. When Jesus departed to the coast of Tyre and Sidon, which are both black nations, He encountered a woman of Canaan. She was a black woman who was a descendant of Ham, by way of Canaan, who came out of the same coast of Tyre and Sidon. She cried unto Him to have mercy on her, calling him the son of David, because her daughter was grievously vexed with a devil. But the Lord did not respond to her. His disciples asked Him to send her away because she keeps crying to us. Jesus responded by saying that He was not sent but to the lost sheep of the house of Israel. This black woman then came worshipping Him, and saying, Lord, help me.

> "But he answered and said, It is not meet to take the children's bread, and to cast it to **dogs**. And she said, Truth, Lord: yet the **dogs** eat of the crumbs which fall from their masters' table. Then Jesus answered and said unto her, O woman, great is thy faith: be it unto thee even as thou wilt. And her daughter was made whole from that very hour" (Matthew 15:26–28).

This same term "**dogs**" is used by the Lord when He instructs His disciples not to give or reveal that which is holy to outsiders or unbelievers. "Give not that which is holy unto the **dogs**, neither cast ye your pearls before swine, lest they trample them under their feet, and turn again and rend you" (Matthew 7:6). Then in the book of the Revelation, the Apostle John says they that do the Lord's commandments are blessed and may have a right to the tree of life, and may enter the gates into the city (See Revelations 22:14). But he went on to say, "For without are **dogs**, and sorcerers, and whoremongers, and murderers, and idolaters, and whosoever loveth and maketh a lie" (Revelation 22:15). (See also Philippians 3:2).

Caleb was evidently a proselyte in Israel that identified with the tribe of Judah because he was sent out as one of the twelve spies representing Judah. "Of the tribe of Judah, Caleb the son of Jephunneh" (Numbers 13:6).

However, other Scriptures give us more detail about Caleb's lineage. Moses was addressing the children of Reuben and the children of Gad's desire to take an inheritance on the other side of Jordan, and he made reference to the children of Israel that didn't want to go up and possess their inheritance, who discouraged the heart of the rest of the children of Israel. Moses said the Lord said, that of those men that came out of Egypt twenty years old and older would not see the land that He swore to Abraham and Isaac and Jacob, because they have not wholly followed the Lord. He went on to say that the only ones who would see the land were, "Caleb the son of Jephunneh the Kenezite and Joshua the son of Nun: for they have wholly followed the Lord" (Numbers 32:12).

Other Scriptures that give evidence of Caleb's lineage are: "Then the children of Judah came unto Joshua in Gilgal: and Caleb the son of Jephunneh the Kenezite said unto him, Thou knowest the thing that the Lord said unto Moses the man of God concerning me and thee in Kadesh-barne-a" (Joshua 14:6). Also, "And Joshua blessed him, and gave unto Caleb the son of Jephunneh Hebron for an inheritance. Hebron therefore became the inheritance of Caleb the son of Jephunneh the Kenezite unto this day, because that he wholly followed the Lord God of Israel" (Joshua 14:13, 14).

The Kenezites come from Kenaz, an Edomite Duke, the son of Esau and Adah, the daughter of Elon the Hittite. "Now these are the generations of Esau, who is Edom. Esau took his wives of the daughters of Canaan; Adah the daughter of Elon the Hittite…" (Genesis 36:1, 2). Adah the Hittite bare Esau one child. "And Adah bare to Esau Eliphaz…" (Genesis 36:4). Then Eliphaz's fifth son was Kenaz who was the father of the Kenezites. "And the sons of Eliphaz were Teman, Omar, Zepho, and Gatam, and Kenaz" (Genesis 36:11). Eliphaz also had a son through his concubine Timna, whose name was Amalek. This son was the father of the Amalekites. Esau had great substance and riches which he got in the land of Canaan; it was so much that he and his family could not dwell together with his brother Jacob. And the land where they were strangers could not bear them because of their cattle. "Thus dwelt Esau in mount Seir: Esau is Edom" (Genesis 36:8). Esau made all of his sons dukes, and Kenaz, the father of the Kenezites, was one of those dukes. "The margin of the King James Bible calls them *commanders*."[3] "These were dukes of the sons of Esau: the sons of Eliphaz the firstborn son of Esau; duke Teman, duke Omar, duke Omar, duke Zepho, duke Kenaz" (Genesis 36:15).

It was Esau's wife Adah the Hittite that bore him Kenaz, the father of the Kenezites. The Hittites evolved from Heth, the son of Canaan, the son of Ham. "And Canaan begat Sidon his firstborn, and Heth, And the Jebusite, and the Amorite, and the Girgasite…" (Genesis 10:15, 16). The margin of the Bible says that "Heth was the father of the Hittites."[4]

Esau also married Aholibamah the daughter of Anah the daughter of Zibeon the Hivite, a descendant of Ham through Canaan. (See Genesis 36:2). Then his third marriage was to Mahalath (Bathshemath) Ishmael's daughter, sister of Nebajoth. (See Genesis 36:3). Remember that Ishmael's mother Hagar was an Egyptian, who was a descendant of Ham by way of his son, Mizraim.

The Edomites (Esau) married into a dark-skinned race, and remember that Hebrews in their natural habitat have olive brown to very dark skin. Caleb, the son of Jephunneh the Kenezite, was a descendant of the duke Kenaz, who came from a union of Esau and Adah, the daughter of Elon, the Hittite, who was a descendant of Canaan, who was the son of Ham. Remember that Ham's name means dark or swarthy, black or warm, and a name in Scripture denotes character and purpose in Scripture.

Caleb was given a part (City of Hebron) among the children of Judah. This is one of the reasons that Caleb represented the tribe of Judah when the twelve spies were sent out. "And unto Caleb the son of Jephunneh he gave a part among the children of Judah, according to the commandment of the Lord to Joshua, even the city of Arba the father of Anak, which city is Hebron" (Joshua 15:13). In the Chronicles of Israel after all the lineage of Judah is named, then the lineage of Caleb is named and the city of Hebron that they were given. (See 1 Chronicles 2:42).

"Although Caleb was not an Israelite by birth, he was 'an Israelite indeed.' He was one of the chief spies sent out by Moses. He was courageous and persevered when the other spies became discouraged. He was invincible in driving out giants, completely devoted to God and vigorous in old age. Six times it is recorded of Caleb, "he hath fully followed the Lord."[5]

"When we come to the record of Caleb's personal inheritance in the land of Canaan we find him at eighty five years of age asking of Joshua, "Now therefore give me this mountain." Caleb was a man of altitudes. He was not content with the average or the commonplace. It was the heights for Caleb, and although the mountain he wanted was filled with hostile Anakims, he refused defeat and claimed his inheritance."[6]

We can see this kind of strength exemplified in the many unspoken-of black heroes that have helped to free and liberate black and poor people from the continued effects of slavery and oppression that have affected the diaspora of the world. Some of the giants of black people who have had a Caleb spirit and helped to liberate people from oppression like, Sojourner Truth, Harriett Tubman, Frederick Douglas, W.E.B Dubois, Horace Mann, Rev. Nathaniel (Nat) Turner, Rev. Dr. Martin Luther King Jr., Medgar Evans, Thurgood Marshall, and Nelson Mandela are known more than many others. But there are myriads of other blacks that are not well known nationally or internationally that function even today under a "Caleb Spirit" to claim the inheritance of freedom for blacks and the poor and the needy across the earth. Black people who work every day, putting their life on the line, still crying out "Give us the mountain of freedom and inheritance that belongs to us."

Othniel – Judge of Israel

A Judge of Israel and Caleb's younger brother – A Kenezite. We have presented extensive truth and facts that "although Caleb was not an Israelite by birth, he was 'an Israelite indeed.'"[7] The same holds true for his younger brother Othniel. "Othniel's name means **force of God**."[8] "His name also means powerful one or lion of God. He was a son of Kenaz, who after the death of Joshua judged Israel for forty years. He is the first to be mentioned among the 'Judges.'"[9]

The nature of this black man, who later became a judge of Israel, is seen in the first mention of him in Israel's history. "The first mention of Othniel is on the occasion of the taking of Kiriath-sepher, or *Debir*, as it was afterward called. Caleb, to whom the city was assigned, offered as a reward to its captor, his daughter Achsah. Othniel won the prize.[10]

> "And Caleb said, He that smiteth Kirjath-sepher, and taketh it, to him will I give Achsah my daughter to wife. And Othniel the son of Kenaz, the brother of Caleb, took it: and he gave him Achsah his daughter to wife" (Joshua 15:16, 17). (See also Judges 1:12, 13).

"Israel 'forgot the Lord their God, and served Baal and Asheroth.' As a punishment for their idolatry the Lord delivered them into the hands of Cushan-rishathaim, king of Mesopotamia, whom they were obliged to serve for eight years. In this oppression the Israelites cried unto the Lord, and He raised them up a deliverer in the person of Othniel the Kenizzite."[11]

> "And the children of Israel dwelt among the Canaanites, Hittites, and Amorites, and Perizzites, and Hivites, and Jebusites: And they took their daughters to be their wives, and gave their daughters to their sons, and served their gods. And the children of Israel did evil in the sight of the Lord and forgat the Lord their God, and served Baalim and the groves. Therefore the anger of the Lord was hot against Israel, and he sold them into the hand of Cushan-rishathaim king of Mesopotamia: and the children of Israel served Cushan-rishathaim eight years. And when the children of Israel cried unto the Lord, the Lord raised up a deliverer to the children of Israel, who delivered them, even Othniel the son of Kenaz, Caleb's younger brother. And the Spirit of the Lord came upon him, and he judged Israel, and went out to war: and the Lord delivered Cushan-rishathaim king

of Mesopotamia into his hand; and his hand prevailed against Cushan-rishathaim. And the land had rest forty years. And Othniel the son of Kenaz died" (Judges 3:5-11).

This black man was actually the first Deliverer/Judge of Israel. The children of Israel served the Lord all the days of Joshua and all the days of the elders that outlived Joshua. These were elders that had known all the works of the Lord that He had done for Israel. After their deaths, the children of Israel did evil in the sight of the Lord and served Baalim and other gods. Then the Lord raised up Deliverer/Judges who would deliver the children of Israel from the other nations and the other gods, and then judge them in the ways of the Lord and their freedom. Othniel was the first of these Deliverer/Judges who kept Israel in the way of the Lord. He happened to be a black man, Caleb's younger brother, a Kenizzite.

"Little is recorded of this saviour who represented the tribe of Judah. He followed the Lord with all his heart, and, Spirit-empowered, he fought for Israel and prevailed."[12] He was not an Israelite by birth, but like his brother Caleb was an Israelite indeed.

Elliott's Commentary for English Readers makes reference to Othniel's birth name: "Othniel is mentioned in Joshua 15:15–17. It is here added that he was Caleb's younger brother. (See Judges 3:9). The Hebrew may mean either that Othniel was "son of Kenaz and brother of Caleb" (in which case he married his niece); or "son of Kenaz, who was Caleb's brother: (as in "Jonadab, the son of Shimeah David's brother," 2 Samuel 13:3), in which case Achsah was his cousin. The Masoretes, to whom is due the punctuation of our Hebrew Scriptures, show by their pointing that they understood the words in the former sense. But though Ben-Kenaz may simply mean Kenezite (Joshua 14:6; Numbers 32:12), it is strange in that case that Othniel should never be called a son of Jephunneh. If he was a brother of Caleb's, he must have lived to extreme old age and have been an old man when he married Achsah. For the importance of Caleb's family, see 1 Chronicles 27:15. The Rabbis identify Othniel with the Jabez who is so abruptly introduced in 1 Chronicles 4:9, 10, and connect Achsah's petition with the prayer there recorded; and they suppose that he founded the school of scribes at Jabez (1 Chronicles 2:55), and was a teacher of law to the Kenites."

The *Targum* says: "Jabez, who was Othniel, was more honored and expert in the Law than his brother; his mother had called his name Jabez, "for," she said, "I gave birth to him in pain." "Jabez prayed to the God of Israel saying: "O that you might indeed bless me with sons," and extend my territory with disciples! O that your hand might be with me in debate, and that you might provide me with companions like myself, so that the evil inclination may not provoke me. And the Lord brought about what he had asked for."

The Jewish Encyclopedia, by Emil G. Hirsh and Kaufmann Kohler, says: "Jabez was prominent, particularly after the Exile, among those Kenite clans that embraced Judaism, becoming scribes and teachers of the Law. Rabbinical tradition identifies Jabez with Othniel the Kenezite, the head of the bet ha-midrash after the death of Moses (Tem. 16a; Targ. to 1 Chron. 2:55, 4:9). Hence the vow of Jabez was understood to refer to his schoolhouse; "If Thou wilt bless me with children, and give me many disciples and associates," etc. (Tem. l.c.; Sanh. 106a). "The whole tribe of Jethro, the Kenites as well as the Rechabites, left their habitations near Jericho and went to Jabez to learn the Torah from him" (Mek., Yitro, "Amalek, 2; Sifre, Num. 78).

Here again we see this black man, who became the first judge of Israel, besides many other prominent positions of notoriety in Israel, was not an Israelite by birth, but identified with the purposes of the God of Israel and rose above His brethren and was a recipient of the blessings of the Lord indeed. He was a black man who was recognized as an Israelite indeed.

Chushan-rishathaim or Chushan-rishathaim – King of Mesopotamia

A king of Mesopotamia, defeated by Othniel, the Kenizzite, the younger brother of Caleb. His name means blackness of iniquities.[13] "Cushan is another form of Cush or perhaps an Arabian country occupied by Cushites."[14] "I saw the tents of Cushan in affliction: and the curtains of the land of Midian did tremble" (Habakkuk 3:7). Cush was the eldest son of Ham, and was the father of Nimrod and many other black nations. Cush means black or Ethiopian.

"Cushan-rishathaim also means **blackness**. He was king of Mesopotamia while Israel commenced to sin before heaven, he was steered by Jehovah to overrun Israel because of her transgressions. He governed her for eight years before being dispossessed by Othniel," Caleb's younger brother.

King Cushan-rishathaim was Israel's first major oppressor following the Exodus. He was Hamitic in origin and a great descendant of the Black man "Cush," the same as Ethiopia.

The Greek Herodotus, of 447 B.C., known as the father of history, clearly stated that the ancient inhabitants of Mesopotamia were Black. The Ethiopians, Persians, and Babylonians, says Herodotus, were of the same family linguistically, ethnographically and historically.

According to Sir Arthur Keith's research on the Mount Carmel excavations for the Royal College of Surgeons, the inhabitants of Persia and southern Mesopotamia seem to have been members of a black-skinned, wide-nosed, and woolly-haired race."[15]

"The attempt to limit ancient Black people to the continent of Africa is done by some modern scholars of ancient history. Nevertheless, the Black people extended their nations and travels far beyond Africa. In Judges 3:8 the holy writers used the term Chushan-rishathaim, to name this ruler of Mesopotamia. The Hebrew from which the English term came was used at that particular time to identify Black people. It is evident that after having left the Black Pharaohs of Egypt, Israel came under the domination of a Black ruler of Mesopotamia."[16] Under Othniel, the Kenizzite, Israel's first judge, Israel defeated this ruler of Mesopotamia.

"Consistently the Israelites dominated and were dominated by foreign powers. During these periods of domination the cohabitation of the races continued. From the entire Books of Judges and of Ruth there are many names of foreign nations that Israel came into contact with on all levels of life."[17]

Notice in the Scriptures that it was the **Lord** that sold Israel into the hand of this black king of Mesopotamia, Chushan-rishathaim. Because of Israel's disobedience the Lord made Israel to serve this king for eight years. Then eventually this king within time "oppressed the Israelites during these eight years."[18] Then the children of Israel cried unto the Lord, and He raised up a deliverer to deliver them.

"And the children of Israel did evil in the sight of the Lord, and forgat the Lord their God, and served Baalim and the groves. Therefore the anger of the Lord was hot against Israel, and he sold them into the hand of Chushan-rishathaim king of Mesopotamia: and the children of Israel served Chushan-rishathaim eight years. And when the children of Israel cried unto the Lord, the Lord raise up a deliverer to the children of Israel, who deliver them, even Othniel the son of Kenaz, Caleb's younger brother (Judges 3:7–9).

Tirhaka – King of Ethiopia

"His name means exalted."[19] "He is also referred as king of Ethiopia, or Cush, and of Egypt."[20] Tirhakah was an Ethiopian prince during Sennacherib's uprising to overthrow King Hezekiah of Judah. He became an ally of Hezekiah to prevent Judah any further harassment by the Assyrians."[21] "This prince, at the head of a powerful army, attempted to relieve Hezekiah, when attacked by Sennacherib, but the Assyrian army was routed before he came up."[22]

"The Judeans at that time were weak, and their military lacked the stamina to sustain Sennacherib's force. Tirhakah out of mercy tried to help Judah by attacking the aggressor, but was unable to annihilate him. Instead, the young prince suffered innumerable casualties that forced him back to Egypt, where he became a temporary ruler through his uncle Shabaka, the acting Pharaoh."[23] "His name appears as Taharka in the Egyptian records. At the time an Ethiopian dynasty was ruling Egypt in the person of Shabaka, not Tirhakah, who did not ascend the throne until 691 B.C., some dozen years later. The explanation is that Tirhakah, mentioned as king (2 Kings 19:9; Isaiah 37:9) actually opposed Sennacherib in 701 B.C., as a high military commander under his uncle, Shabaka, who was the ruling Pharaoh. Whether the nephew had the status of a regent at the time, or whether the Judean analyst wrote proleptically, is not known."[24]

"He is undoubtedly the Taracus of Manetho, and the Tearch of Strabo, the third and last king of the twenty-fifth or Ethiopian dynasty. It is supposed that he is the Pharaoh intended in Isaiah 30:2," which is a rebuke to Israel for depending on Egypt. "That walk to go down into Egypt, and have not asked at my mouth; to strengthen themselves in the strength of Pharaoh, and to trust in the shadow of Egypt!" (Isaiah 30:2)." Isaiah 19 depicts the anarchy which succeeded his reign. He was a powerful monarch, ruling both Upper and Lower Egypt, and extending his conquests far into Asia and towards the "pillars of Hercules" in the West"[25]

"Against Esarhaddon he was initially victorious, but three years later (670 B.C.) he was defeated, expelled from Memphis, and never returned. He maintained himself in Upper Egypt until his death in 663 B.C., when the Twenty –sixth Dynasty took over"[26]

"Tirhakah's glorious rule won him notoriety, as the Jews watched him galloping across the battlefield to aid Hezekiah. The Egyptians and Ethiopians loved and never forgot him, and even Esarhaddon, in honor of Tirhakah, had his portrait engraved on a stele in Sinjirli. The diplomatic and military prowess of Tirhakah was long remembered and respected."[27] "His name and victories are recorded on an ancient temple at Medinet Abou, in Upper Egypt."[28]

"So Rabshakeh returned and found the king of Assyria warring against Libnah: for he had heard that he was departed from Lachish. And when he heard say of Tirhakah king of Ethiopia, Behold, he is come out to fight against thee: he sent messengers again unto Hezekiah, saying, Thus shall ye speak to Hezekiah king of Judah, saying, Let not thy God in whom thou trustiest deceive thee, saying, Jerusalem shall not be delivered into the hand of the king of Assyria" (2 Kings 19:8–10). (See also Isaiah 37:9).

This black king of Ethiopia, Tirhakah, earned a notable place in history in the world, and a very special place in the history of Israel.

Zephaniah – The Prophet

His name means "Jehovah is Darkness or God Hides. He is a *son of Cushi*, who prophesied in the days of Josiah (Zephaniah 1:1). The prophet Zephaniah gives us a minute account of his genealogy – a rare thing for a prophet! Possibly he pursued this course for two reasons:

    To distinguish himself from three others of the same name.

    To point out his relation to the great monarch, Hezekiah. The Hizkiah of Zephaniah 1:1 is identical with King Hezekiah. Zephaniah was therefore of royal descent."[29]

"Zephaniah, the son of Ethiopia (Cushi), was a royal figure and Judah's ninth prophet prior to the reign of King Josiah. He was a sensitive man who opposed outside customs, which were decaying Judah's religion. Zephaniah tried persistently to awaken Judah about future catastrophes through which all nations would be punished for their negligence to observe God! He was one of the last Old Testament prophets to preach punctiliously.

Zephaniah was from the lineage of Hezekiah, a great descendant of Black Jezebel through her daughter who married into the Davidic line; possibly his great-great-grandson."[30]

> "The word of the Lord which came unto Zephaniah the son of Cushi, the son Gedaliah, the son of Amariah, the son of Hizkiah (Hezekiah), in the days of Josiah the son of Amon, king of Judah" (Zephaniah 1:1).

"The constant contact of the Hebrew people with the Black people resulted in the development of Black prophets. Zephaniah was a descendant of a Black father.

The acceptance of Black people into the Hebrew nation was evidently a normal practice. The holy writer used the term Cushi which definitely distinguished Zephaniah as being a black man. Nevertheless, he saw himself as being a part of the Hebrew nation.

He prophesied as a prophet of Israel. "Ye Ethiopians also, ye shall be slain by my sword." "From beyond the rivers of Ethiopia my suppliants, even the daughter of my dispersed, shall bring mine offering."

Zephaniah was acquainted with his Black people. The Hebrew terms from which the English terms "Cushi" and "Ethiopia" came have the same Hebrew root word. It is peculiar that the translators of Zephaniah 1:1 would use the term "Cushi" rather than the term "an Ethiopian."

In Zephaniah 2:12 and 3:10 the terms which came from the root word *Kush* were translated "Ethiopians" and "Ethiopia." Nevertheless, the Hebrew term revealed the Black identity of Zephaniah. In Zechariah 6:10 reference was made to the prophet Zephaniah and Zechariah 6:14 reference was made to Hen who was the son of Zephaniah. After the book of Zephaniah, the references to Black people decreased, as did the books of the Old Testament. Around 586 B.C., the Babylonians conquered Jerusalem. The Hebrews remained under the dominance of the Babylonians until 538 B.C. In around 538 B.C. the Hebrews returned to Jerusalem. The period of history from 538 B.C. to about A.D. 3 was not comprehensively included in the Old Testament canon. Therefore, the New Testament is the source to be studied for Black biblical characters and references during the Apostolic Age."[31]

Zerah – The Ethiopian Warrior/King

"His name means sprout or springing up of light."[32] "His name is also referenced to mean dawning, rising or shining. He is referred to as the Ethiopian (or Cushite) king defeated by Asa. After a period of ten years' peace, Asa's reign was disturbed by war. Zerah, with a million men and three hundred chariots, invaded the kingdom and pressed forward to Mareshah.[33]

"During the reign of King Asa, the Ethiopians came from Ethiopia to Palestine. The Ethiopians were known to be great warriors: therefore, King Asa feared the Ethiopians. Black Zerah and his men put up a good battle. The Black ruler had led his men a long distance to Palestine; however, Black Zerah lost the battle. Black Zerah however was a great warrior."[34] In Scripture, God made reference to the greatness of this Warrior/King. "Were not the Ethiopians and the Lubims a huge host, with very many chariots and horsemen? Yet, because thou didst rely on the Lord, he delivered them into thine hand" (II Chronicles 16:8).

"Not much more is recorded about the great Ethiopian General Zerah. He led the invasion of Judah against Asa around 900 B.C. Despite the scarcity of information, it is certain that he marched into Judah with a million men. The armies met on a final battlefield at Mareshah. Asa faced the African with a much smaller army but it was powerful. He had 300,000 bowmen and men armed with spears and swords. These had come out of Judah. He had thousands of heavily armed soldiers who came from Benjamin."[35]

However, Zerah, the Ethiopian commander's vast army "signified Ethiopia's sovereignty during King Asa's reign of Judah. Zerah was well known for his superior tactics and numerous conquests. There is much suspicion that he overcame many cities with this vast army, which was well-organized and highly disciplined. When Judah was enjoying her long period of peace, Zerah felt it was time to upset her comfort by making war with Asa. The two Kings met in a valley at Mareshah, and there they clashed! Zerah the Ethiopian immediately crippled Asa's strength, which made a victory seem impossible for the Judean. Asa knew his army was being smashed, so he frantically cried to God for spiritual support. This cry moved God to smote the Ethiopians, whereupon Zerah and his army became so confused that they fled the valley, leaving great spoils before Judah.[36]

"Asa pursued the fleeing Ethiopians as far as Gerar, crippling them so that they could not recover and again make a stand. Some scholars identify Zerah with one of the Osorkons of the Twenty-second or Bubastite Dynasty, particularly with Osorkon (924–895 B.C.), successor of Shishak. However, the reference may simply be to an Arab invasion, since the name Zerah occurs in Arab, inscriptions.[37]

"The Colored Ethiopians, the Negro-Egyptian Hagar and her half-Colored son Ishmael were the original parents of the Arabic people and nations; Arabia's earliest ancestors were people of the Negro race. Thus, study is proving that ancient and modern Arabia's Negro-mixture is indisputable.

This great Ethiopian war strategist can be compared to the Egyptian Pharaoh Ramesses; they both pushed their luck beyond their limits. The legendary Zerah is also recognized by scholars as having once conquered and ruled Egypt as Pharaoh."[38]

> "And there came out against them Zerah the Ethiopian with an host of a thousand thousand, and three hundred chariots; and came unto Mareshah. Then Asa went out against him, and they set the battle in array in the valley of Zephathah at Mareshah. And Asa cried unto the Lord his God, and said, Lord it is nothing with thee to help, whether with many, or with them that have no power: help us, O Lord our God; for we rest on thee, and in thy name we go against this multitude, O Lord, thou art our God; let not man prevail against thee. So the Lord smote the Ethiopians before Asa and before Judah; and the Ethiopians fled. And Asa and the people that were with him pursued them unto Gerar: and the Ethiopians were overthrown that they could not recover

themselves; for they were destroyed (broken) before the Lord, and before his host; and they carried away very much spoil. And they smote all the cities round about Gerar for the fear of the Lord came upon them: and they spoiled all the cities; for there was exceeding much spoil in them. They smote also the tents of cattle, and carried away sheep and camels in abundance, and returned to Jerusalem" (II Chronicles 14:9–15).

---

1 Strong, James H. *Strong's Exhaustive Concordance.*
2 Lockyer, Herbert. *All the Men of the Bible*, p. 82.
3 *King James Version of the Bible (The).* Thomas Nelson Publishers.
4 *Ibid.*
5 Lockyer, Herbert. *All the Men of the Bible*, p. 82.
6 *Ibid.*, p. 83.
7 Lockyer, Herbert. *All the Men of the Bible*, p. 82.
8 Strong, James H. *Strong's Exhaustive Concordance*
9 Lockyer, Herbert. *All the Men of the Bible*, p. 266.
10 Unger, Merrill F. *Unger's Bible Dictionary*, p. 949.
11 *Ibid.*
12 Lockyer, Herbert. *All the Men of the Bible*, p. 266.
13 *Ibid.*, p. 85.
14 Unger, Merrill F. *Unger's Bible Dictionary*, p. 267.
15 Johnson, John L. *The Black Biblical Heritage*, p. 95.
16 Rhoades, F. S. *Black Characters and References of the Holy Bible*, p. 41.
17 *Ibid.*, p, 43.
18 *International Bible Dictionary (The)*, p. 93, 94.
19 Lockyer, Herbert. *All the Men of the Bible*, p. 330.
20 *International Bible Dictionary (The)*, p. 464.
21 Johnson, John L. *The Black Biblical Heritage*, p. 189.
22 *International Bible Dictionary (The)*, p. 464.
23 Johnson, John L. *The Black Biblical Heritage*, p. 189.
24 Unger, Merrill F. *Unger's Bible Dictionary*, p. 1289.
25 *International Bible Dictionary (The)*, p. 464.
26 Unger, Merrill F. *Unger's Bible Dictionary*, p. 1289.
27 Johnson, John L. *The Black Biblical Heritage*, p. 189.
28 *International Bible Dictionary (The)*, p. 464.
29 Lockyer, Herbert. *All the Men of the Bible*, p. 346, 347.
30 Johnson, John L. *The Black Biblical Heritage*, p. 195.

Black Leaders in the Bible – Old Testament

31 Rhoades, F.S. *Black Characters and References of the Holy Bible*, p. 72, 73.
32 Lockyer, Herbert. *All the Men of the Bible*, p. 348.
33 Unger, Merrill F. *Unger's Bible Dictionary*, p. 1385.
34 Rhoades, F. S. *Black Characters and References of the Holy Bible*, p. 55
35 Hyman, Mark. *Blacks Who Died for Jesus*, p. 96.
36 Johnson, John L. *The Black Biblical Heritage*, p. 187.
37 Unger, Merrill F. *Unger's Bible Dictionary*, p. 1385.
38 Johnson, John L. *The Black Biblical Heritage*, p. 187.

CHAPTER 9

Black Women in the Bible – Old Testament

Zipporah – Moses' Wife

"A Midian name that means 'a sparrow.'"[1] Her name also means, "little bird"[2] and also means "beauty."[3]

"Moses crossed beyond the Red Sea, deep into the Sinai Peninsula. At length he came to a well, and oasis in a parched land. He paused to refresh himself, and while he was there a group of women came up to the well to draw water for their flocks. Seven in all, they were sisters, the daughters of a priest of Midian. The Midianites, it will be recalled, were descendants of Abraham by his second wife, Keturah. Moses, of course, was a descendant of Abraham also, by his first wife, Sarah.

As the women were drawing water for their father's herd, certain shepherds came on the scene and summarily demanded the right to draw water ahead of the women. Apparently this had happened quite often, and the women had perforce yielded. But this time Moses offered himself as their champion. Though they were strangers to him, he could not sit by and see them mistreated by chauvinists. He defended their rights, made the shepherds wait, and helped the sisters water their animals.

Their chore finished, the women drove their herd home, where they surprised their father by arriving so early in the day. They explained how a stranger, "an Egyptian" (for Moses was still dressed in the garments he customarily wore in Egypt), had helped them. The father sent the women back to invite Moses to lodge in their home.

This man is variously known as Jethro, Reuel, or Raguel. As a priest of Midian, he was distinguished from other Midianites in that he worshiped only one God. No doubt this belief had been handed down through his family line from Abraham, although it had died out among most of his kinsmen. At any rate, it harmonized exactly with Moses; own faith, and he apparently felt at home with this nomad of the desert.

Moses remained with Jethro forty years, spending the time tending Jethro's flocks. The latter gave him a daughter for his wife."[4]

> "And Moses was content to dwell with the man: and he gave Moses Zipporah his daughter. And she bare him a son, and he called his name Gershom: for he said I have been a stranger in a strange land" (Exodus 2:21, 22).

Moses was under this priest for 40 years. Jethro's name means excellency. This black priest had an innate spirit of excellency that needed to be imparted to Moses. This priest along with his daughters already knew God and had a one-God concept of faith. He was a priest serving the Most High God upon the mountain. Moses learned as an assistant shepherd under his daughter Zipporah, who became his wife. Zipporah was already functioning as a shepherdess when he met her.

"Black Jethro received Moses, a fugitive from the unjust systems of Black Egypt, as a fellow human being. 'And Moses was content to dwell with the man: and he gave Moses Zipporah his daughter.'

Black Jethro who saw all men as children of God accepted Moses as his son-in-law. Moses' wife, Black Zipporah, was a Black beauty who had developed the same religious beliefs that her father had developed. Zipporah did not worship idols. She believed in an unseen God who was Spirit. She helped Moses to develop his faith in God. Her faith precipitated Moses' decision to inquire about the God of Black Jethro, the God of the mountain.

Some writers have taken the relationship of Moses and Black Zipporah out of its proper historical context. Looking at Numbers 12:1, we find the following words:

> "And Miriam and Aaron spake against Moses because of the Ethiopian woman whom he had married: for he had married an Ethiopian woman."

One scholar said that the modern Jews felt embarrassed because Moses had a Black wife. Modern thinking about Blacks may have produced such feeling. However, the ancient Black people could have felt some embarrassment. Moses was a member of the Hebrew people, who were disgraced in slavery under Black masters. Moses was the outcast who was like a runaway slave in A.D. 1850. If anyone should have been embarrassed, Jethro and Zipporah, free and prosperous Blacks, should have been embarrassed. Today, the Jews should not be embarrassed. Only the Black people, if anyone, should respond with bad feelings about Black Zipporah's marriage to a murderer and a fugitive. However, the faith of Black Zipporah in a just God who saw all of His human beings as equals helped her to be a true wife of Moses. Black Zipporah became one with Moses, and she made the sacrifices that were essential in helping Moses lead his people out of slavery. From her Black body she gave Moses Black children."[5]

"Moses had been specially selected by God to deliver the Hebrews from Egyptian bondage. Nevertheless, on several occasions he experienced rebellion in the ranks. One of these was led by his own brother and sister.

Aaron and Miriam took as their point of departure the fact that, as the King James Version reads, Moses "had married an Ethiopian woman" (Numbers 12:1). Other versions say he had married a Cushite woman. Bible students differ in their interpretations of this. Some say this must refer to a second wife, since the book of Exodus details Zipporah as a Midianite. In fact, Josephus, a secular Jewish historian of the first century, A.D., avers that Moses had married a princess named Tharbis, of Meroe, south of Cush, before the Exodus.

But Jewish expositors, and probably the majority of Christian commentators, disagree with this. First, there is no evidence that Zipporah had died or that Moses had married a second time. Second, there was a branch of Cush on the eastern coast of the Red Sea, even as there had been a branch in Mesopotamia. It may be that the Midianites intermingled with these Cushites and that Zipporah had a Cushite as well as a Midianite heritage. In Habakkuk 3:7, Cushan and Midian are named together, as though they shared a geographical identity.

The term "Cushite" may have been nonspecific in Hebrew usage, even as "Ethiopian" was in Greek. To the ancient Greeks, "Ethiopian" meant anyone of a dark complexion, regardless of his birthplace. They wrote of the Ethiopians "where the sun rose," and

Ethiopians "where the sun went down." They even felt that the gods favored those people of "the sun-burnt faces," going to their country for vacations—if the gods take vacations.

Later the Greeks (Herodotus in particular) began to differentiate between "Ethiopian with straight black hair," probably referring to dark people of Arabia and India, and "Ethiopians with wooly black hair." Then they limited their usage of the term to those people who lived south of Egypt. As is much evidenced by their paintings, sculpture, and pottery, the Greeks certainly included Negroes among the "Ethiopians."

Aaron and Miriam probably were not so much opposed to the color of Moses' wife, or even to the fact that he had married outside their race, as their stated objective specified. Their hero, Joseph, had married an Egyptian. In addition, there were many Egyptians accompanying the Hebrews on their trek, either as married relations or as converts to their religion. Eventually, these were absorbed into the Israelite nation.

Miriam and Aaron were simply jealous of their brother. But they used a familiar racist theme to express this disaffection. The Lord drastically punished the pair. Miriam, the ring-leader, came down with the dreaded disease leprosy. Only after Moses personally pled with the Lord on her behalf was she healed, but much chastened."[6]

"The Black race not only educated Moses for the responsible duties to which he was to be ultimately called by Jehovah, but it also gave him a lawfully wedded wife. There is much food for thought, in these days of racial discrimination, and of old legislation against miscegenation, to contemplate the fact that this great lawgiver, who used to commune with the Almighty on Mount Sinai; who also received the two tables of stone on which the Decalogue had been engraved by the finger of God, was not ashamed to take an Ethiopian woman to be his wife."[7]

"It is very plain from the narrative of the entire chapter of Numbers 12, (which the Holy Spirit must have constrained Moses to place on record, although distinctly disadvantageous to his own brother and sister), that God is bitterly opposed to prejudice based on racial lines. Otherwise, what would become of the "Fatherhood of God, and the Brotherhood of Man"? Hath not one God and Father made us all? Then again let us surmise the reasons why He did not vouchsafe the petition which Moses had made on behalf of his stricken sister. Is it because God wished to make hers a public example and warning to those stiff-necked people who was the cause of Moses losing his patience, and as a consequence, of his being deprived the privilege of entering the "Promised Land"? If his own blood relatives did not hesitate to find fault with him because of his Black wife whom he had married, it would not take long before their pernicious example would be followed by the multitude at large, whose jeers and taunts would make the life of this saintly man, and that of his wife, one of constant humiliation. But with the divine affliction and punishment that had been meted out to Miriam, the respect due to the wife of Moses would be forever assured.

In conclusion, the Black race should feel proud that one of its daughters had been considered as worthy to be the wedded companion of the author of the Pentateuch, and that God Almighty had interposed directly and personally, in her behalf, so as to secure to her the respect that she was entitled to, irrespective of her dark, pigmented skin."[8]

"This experience should be an object lesson to anyone who would categorize his fellow man on various levels of moral worth, based solely on his color or ethnic background. With the God who made man, "there is no respect of persons" (Roman 2:11); that is, He does not value one class of humanity as inherently superior to another. So why should we?"[9]

Even recently, in religious circles that I usually flow in, this color prejudice became a great issue that divided a church movement.

The son of a founding father in the faith in Spirit-filled circles became the next leader defacto after the father passed. In the Bible School of this movement, the son, lecturing said, we are glad to have so many blacks that are a part of our Bible School. However, though we teach them and work with them, we don't marry them. While his wife tried to hush him and re-direct this statement, he protested no, let me explain! If we marry blacks, we will wipe them out as a race, he said.

How ignorant this prejudice and this statement were, with him not knowing that the black gene is dominant. That is, usually when one mates with a black person, the offspring comes out as a child of color.

The most popular black minister in that circle responded with a 7-page letter saying he could no longer support a ministry and movement that sees blacks as inferior or less than other races. He went on to say that he could no longer minister at the annual camp meeting for that movement in good conscious. He stated that I know that you see me as the exception, but I can no longer be your exception. He continued by saying, the tens of thousands of dollars that I give to the camp meetings annually I can no longer give in good conscience recognizing that you see blacks as inferior based on the color of their skin.

This rift lasted in this movement for many years and affected the whole Body of Christ in the USA.

Then on a particular island in the Caribbean, an old-line Pentecostal denomination had many more Black pastors than Indian pastors. The Indian congregants did not want their children to marry other blacks, Christian or otherwise. If they did, these Christian would disinherit their children. Then the Indian congregants would not let the Black Pastors affiliate at their weddings, or funerals, or baptism because they were black.

I'm sorry to say that today among God's people, the lesson God gave us concerning Zipporah, and the color of her skin, has not been learned as yet by a lot of the church world.

Keturah – Abraham's 2nd Wife

Keturah – Abraham's 2nd Wife – "her name means incense."[10]

> "Then again Abraham took a wife, and her name was Keturah. And she bore him Zimran, and Jokshan, and Medan, and Midian, and Ishbak, and Shuah. And Jokshan begat Sheba and Dedan. And the sons of Dedan were Asshurim, and Letushim, and Leummim. And the sons of Midian; Ephah, and Epher, and Hanoch, and Abidah, and Eldaah. All these were the children of Keturah. And Abraham gave all that he had unto Isaac, But unto the sons of the concubines, which Abraham had, Abraham gave gifts, and sent them away from Isaac his son while he yet lived, eastward unto the east country" (Genesis 25:1–6).

Keturah is a black woman whose name is associated with incense from Southeast Arabia. One of her and Abraham's six sons, Midian, was the founder of the Midianites. The Midianites must have had a close association with the Ishmaelites (offspring of Abraham and his concubine Hagar) because their names are used interchangeably. (See Genesis 37:25, 28, 36; Genesis 39:1; Judges 8:22, 24). They evidently had a close association with Egypt as they sold Joseph to Potiphar, an officer of Pharaoh. Also, Ethiopia at that time was southern Egypt, and from time to time Ethiopian Pharaoh's ruled the Egyptian Empire which also included Lybia

(Lubim). They had close relations with the descendants of Hagar's son – Ishmael. (See also Habakkuk 3:7; Exodus 2:15, 16; Exodus 3:1; Numbers 12:1; Numbers 10:29; Judges 1:16; Judges 4:11; 1 Samuel 15:6; 1 Chronicles 2:55)

"The Bible does not record Keturah's circumstances of birth, but she may well have been an Egyptian as was Hagar. On the other hand, "Keturah" is similar to an Arabian word for incense, and so she may have come from the southeast area of Arabia, where incense was a chief stock in trade.

Keturah bore Abraham six sons, and perhaps daughters as well. The Biblical record follows the fortunes of only one of them, Midian, and infers that his people were of a darker pigmentation. All but one of Abraham's children by Keturah settled in the Sinai Peninsula or other parts of Arabia."[11]

"Her name is like Kezia, a perfume name. She became the mother of Abraham's six sons: who became the progenitors of six Arabian tribes of Southern and Eastern Palestine. Ancient Israelites regarded the Arabs as distant relatives. The patriarch in his declining years was surrounded by a woman's care and love, and a circle of dear children.[12] "Through the offspring of Keturah, Abraham became the 'father of a multitude of nations'."[13]

Hagar, The Egyptian – Abraham's Concubine

"Hagar, an Egyptian name, closely resembles the root of the Arabic word, *flight*, familiar to us as the history of Mohammed, a descendant of Hagar. It may be taken as an adaptation of her original name to the principal circumstances of her life, and understood to mean, *fugitive* or *immigrant*, which Hagar became."[14]

"Hagar was an inhabitant of upper Egypt. The patriarch Abraham lived in Egypt for a season. "And there was a famine in the land: And Abram went down into Egypt to sojourn there; for the famine was grievous in the land" (Genesis 12:10).

While he was in Egypt, Abraham acquired Black Hagar as his maid; later through Sarah's request, he married Hagar. "And Sarai, Abram's wife, took Hagar, her maid the Egyptian, after Abram had dwelt ten years in the land of Canaan, and gave her to her husband Abram to be his wife" (Genesis 16:3). Black Hagar gave Abraham a Black son,"[15]

"This was at a time when Sarah's barrenness posed a serious problem to Abraham. She knew this was a source of great sorrow to her husband, and so she suggested he follow a custom that was fairly common in Mesopotamia, the country of her birth. That is, that he father a child by her personal servant. Sarah would aid at the childbirth, and that, according to the custom, would legitimize the child as Abraham's heir. Laws dating back to Hammurabi covered such situations as this."[16] In the Hebrew culture, the custom would also have Sarah to sit on the birthing stool with Hagar in her lap, thereby feeling much of the pain and agony of childbirth herself.

"This Egyptian woman, Hagar, probably had accompanied Abraham and Sarah when they had returned from their stay in Egypt. The plan was carried out, and Hagar conceived. But she soon developed an overbearing attitude toward her childless mistress, or so Sarah thought, at least. Sarah couldn't put up with that, and the situation became so untenable that Hagar ran away.

The Bible records, however, that this daughter of Egypt had a very special experience. As she wandered in the wilderness, the Lord of heaven visited her. He told her to return to Abraham and Sarah, and that he would bless the fruit of her womb. She would bear a son, the progenitor of a great nation. God even told Hagar what to call her son – Ishmael.[17]

At this venture, I want to dismiss the traditional myth that is usually associated with the character of Hagar as unfavorable. "She was a wonderful woman, who pre-eminently enjoyed God's favor, and deservedly so. A close study of the chronological factors will explain, satisfactorily, to the most scrupulous critic, the Divine favor and consideration so spontaneously bestowed on this humble daughter of Ham, regardless of her mental status.

Chronologically, we learn that for ten years she had been living a spotless life in the home of the "Father of the faithful" before the untoward event, not of her own volition or seeking, which ultimately besmirched her previously immaculate chastity.

"And Sarai, Abram's wife, took Hagar, her maid, the Egyptian, after Abram had dwelt ten years in the land of Canaan, and gave her to Abram her husband to be his wife." (Genesis 16:3). What a record of single-eyed service, and of unsullied character which challenges modern domestic standards.

Is it any wonder, that, the All-seeing Eye of Providence, fully aware of the fact that Hagar could have pleaded "as before Him innocency was found in me" (Daniel 6:22), did not lose any time in delegating an angelic messenger with words of comfort?

Four times did the ambassador of God speak to Hagar words of cheer, or divine solicitude of prophetic reassurance!

> "And the angel of the Lord found her by a fountain of water in the wilderness, by the fountain in the way to Shur. And he said, Hagar, Sarai's maid, whence camest thou? And whither wilt thou go? And she said I flee from the face of my mistress Sarai. And the angel of the Lord said unto her, Return to thy mistress and submit thyself under her hands, and the angel of the Lord said unto her, I will multiply thy seed exceedingly, that it shall not be

numbered for multitude. And the angel of the Lord said unto her, Behold, thou art with child, and shalt bear a son, and shall call his name Ishmael; because the Lord has heard thy affliction" (Genesis 16:7–11).

"The Heavenly messenger was authorized to deliver a prophecy similar to the only other one on record in the Bible, and which was repeated to the Virgin Mother of God's only Begotten Son, thousands of years later:

"Behold thou art with child, and shalt bear a son, and shalt call his name Ishmael, because the Lord hath heard thy affliction" (Genesis 16:11) compared with Luke 1:31.

Hagar, a humble woman of the race of Ham, had "found favor with God" even as had the Virgin Mary (Luke 1:30).

And yet more! A heaven-sent name had been chosen for the unborn Hamitic progeny, even as had been done in ages past, for Isaac (Genesis 17:19); for Cyrus (Isaiah 44:28; 45:1); and for John the Baptist (Luke 1:13).

Was it the angel Gabriel that was sent from God with the divine message to Hagar as he subsequently did to Zacharias (Luke 1:19), and to Mary (Luke 1:26)? Furthermore, we are taught that "God heareth not sinners" (John 9:31). Would God have so honored this daughter of Ham had she not been living a life of unsullied chastity during the ten years she had previously spent in the home of Abraham?

How could Hagar, realizing the pure nature of God refrain from exclaiming; "Thou God seest me!" (Genesis 16:13).

But is this all of Hagar? By no means! Chronology again informs us that "Abram was fourscore and six years old, when Hagar bore Ishmael" (Genesis 16:16). And, furthermore: "Abraham was ninety years and nine – and Ishmael thirteen years old – on the self-same day in which father and son were both circumcised" (Genesis 17:24–26). And again: "And Abraham was an hundred years old, when his son Isaac was born unto him (Genesis 2:55). Ishmael had therefore attained to his fourteenth anniversary.

Fourteen years, or more, had elapsed since Hagar yielded to the unsolicited advances of her master. And twenty-four years, nearly a quarter of a century, had come and gone since she had been in their home! Only one child was born to her!

No clandestine relations ever recurred, to her credit and also to that of the aged patriarch. Birth control was unknown in those days! And, as a challenging proof that Hagar had voluntarily resumed her pristine life of chastity, Divine Providence intervenes on her behalf, and that of her fourteen-year-old Ishmael, which they were compelled to leave the home in which they had lived for nearly a quarter of a century!

Most Bible students are familiar with the trivial incident, probably due to some boyish prank, which provoked the anger of Sarai.

Holy Writ relates graphically this second intervention of God, which thereby proved, beyond dispute, that Hagar was still held in high esteem in the Council of God. And even as he had opened the eyes of Abram, to see the ram caught in the thicket, so did he open Hagar's eyes, to see a well of water!

To quote:

> "And the water was spent in the bottle, and she cast the child under one of the shrubs. And she went, and sat her down over against him a good way off, as it were a bowshot: for she said, Let me not see the death of the child. And she sat over against him, and lifted up her voice, and wept. And God heard the voice of the lad; and the angel of God called to Hagar out of heaven and said unto her, What aileth thee, Hagar? Fear not; for God hath heard the voice of the lad where he is. Arise, lift up the lad, and hold

him in thine hand; for I will make him a great nation. And God opened her eyes and she saw a well of water; and she went, and filled the bottle with water, and gave the lad to drink. And God was with the lad: and he grew, and dwelt in the wilderness, and became an archer" (Genesis 21:15–20).

What divine consideration paid a lowly daughter born under Africa's (the land of Ham) torrid sun! In this biblical record of the life of Hagar, the Egyptian maid there is a lesson to be learned contrary to the negative commentaries of the Western World – "God heareth not sinners."[18]

"Ishmael grew to manhood in the desert, turning out to be even more of a nomad than his father. His mother, herself an Egyptian, found an Egyptian wife for him, and so the Ishmaelite nation was founded, part Semite but heavily Egyptian or Hamitic. They would, of course, be a people of dark complexion, like the Egyptians. They made the northern reaches of the Arabian peninsula their territory."[19]

Asenath – Joseph's African Wife

Asenath is "an Egyptian name implying, one who belongs to Neit the heathen goddess of wisdom, of Sais."[20] "Neit was the Egyptian Minerva."[21] "Three times over Asenath is spoken of as 'the daughter of Potipherah, priest of On.' This priest was associated with the 'Great Temple of the Sun' at Heliopolis, near to modern Cairo. She became the wife of Joseph, Egypt's great deliverer.

The marriage Pharaoh arranged between Joseph and Asenath revealed his determination to identify Joseph completely with Egyptian life. Joseph had become a most valuable man in the land of Egypt and was next to Pharaoh in power. Among the honors he lavished upon Joseph was a marriage into a cast of priest ranking high in Egypt. These were the Sages trained in the wisdom of Egypt (Acts 7:22), and by his marriage to the daughter of one of these Sages, Joseph became assimilated with the priestly caste. As Kuyper expresses it in *Women of the Old Testament*—

Joseph's marriage was a diplomatic arrangement, designated by Pharaoh to place him inside a strictly delineated, aristocratic society, and thus covert him into a naturalized Egyptian."²²

"Egyptians were skilled in architecture and mathematics. The granite pyramids were built early in the third millennium B.C., and demonstrate a high degree of engineering skill. They mined sandstone, copper, manganese, turquoise, beryl, gold, gypsum, and phosphate.

During this period, the third millennium B.C., much of Nubia (another name for Cush) to the south of Egypt was under Egyptian influence, if not under its control. Quite probably, in earlier times there was probably no appreciable differentiation between Egypt and Nubia—the peoples mingled freely. But eventually, a distinction developed. The Egyptians were of a dark hue and black-haired, but the Nubians seem to have been of an ever darker complexion, and some were said to have had wooly hair.

The Egyptians eventually distinguished themselves from the Nubians by calling the latter Negroes. In fact, there is some dispute over whether Egypt was not originally Negro and only replaced by those whose ancestry included a mingling of Asiatic peoples. A noted Senegalese writer of modern times asserts that 'the Egyptian experiment was essentially Negro, and all Africans can draw the same moral advantage from it that Westerners draw from Graeco-Latin civilization.

Abraham visited Egypt in about the eighteenth century B.C. when there was no central government. Instead, local princes ruled, each calling themselves 'Pharaoh.' Even so, Egyptian influence was strong throughout Canaan and as far as Phoenicia.[23]

"Jacob had twelve sons, and he was partial toward his son Joseph. "Now Israel loved Joseph more than all his children, because he was the son of his old age: and he made him a coat of many colors (Genesis 37:3, RSV).

Joseph's brothers became jealous of him. His brothers sold him to a group of Ishmaelites who in turn brought Joseph down to Egypt and sold him to Potiphar to be his slave."[24]

"At the time Joseph arrived in Egypt as a slave, the land was ruled by foreigners, the Hyksos, many of whom may have had a Semitic background. That would help to explain how Joseph, himself as a Semite, could be elevated to so high a position in this land. The story of his elevation, and how he brought his father's family, which settled in Goshen,"[25] is an important part of Hebrew history.

"According to Genesis 41:1, in Black Egypt, there lived a Black priest whose name was Potipherah. He was a God-fearing man, and his household loved God. Pharaoh was well acquainted with this Black priest and with his family. To please Joseph, Pharaoh gave Joseph the beautiful Black daughter of the Black priest, Black Asenath. Joseph was glad to accept this Black woman as his wife and as the future mother of his children. "And Pharaoh called Joseph's name Zaphnath-paaneah; and he gave him to wife Asenath, the daughter of Potipherah, priest of On. And Joseph went out over all the land of Egypt" (Genesis 41:45, RSV)."

Black Asenath and Joseph were blessed with Black children."[26] "By Asenath, the daughter of this eminent priestly family, he had two sons, Manasseh and Ephraim. The descendants of these two sons, who thus had Egyptian heritage and characteristics, became two of the twelve tribes of Israel."[27]

"Around the 5th century, A.D., there was an effort to attach Asenath as the heroine of a remarkable Jewish and heathen romance, in which she renounced her false gods before her marriage."[28]

"Sufficient has been said to establish the fact that the Egyptians of the days of the Pharaohs, were of the race of Ham, and not a branch of the Aryan group. We have both the testimony of the inspired word of God, and that of Herodotus, the Father of History. Therefore, in these days of affected race superiority, when men seem to forget, perhaps too conveniently, that 'of ONE blood hath God made ALL nations,' it may come as a surprise to many to learn that Joseph, who became the Prime Minister of Egypt, married an African/Black woman."[29]

> "And Pharaoh said unto Joseph, I am Pharaoh, and without thee shall no man lift up his hand or foot in all the land of Egypt. And Pharaoh called Joseph's name Zaphnath-paaneah; and he gave him to wife Asenath the daughter of Potipherah, priest of On" (Genesis 41:44, 45).

By the way "Zaphnath-paaneah" means man of food during famine,"[30] and a revealer of secrets.

"As a result of the miscegenation, it must be plain to those who elect to see disgrace and shame in such marriages, that Ephraim and Manasseh, the sons of Joseph, had considerable of the so-called 'Negro-blood' in their veins. They were mulattoes!

> "And unto Joseph were born two sons before the years of famine came, which Asenath the daughter of Potipherah priest of On bare unto him. And Joseph called the name of the first-born Manasseh: For God, said he, hath made me forget all my toil, and all my father's house. And the name of the second called he Ephraim: For God hath caused me to be fruitful in the land of my affliction" (Genesis 41:50–52).

Did the patriarch Jacob despise these negroid off-springs which had been grafted into the stock of Israel, God's chosen people? Let us turn to the Holy Bible again for the answer:

> "And it came to pass after these things, that one told Joseph, Behold, thy father is sick: and he took with him his two sons Manasseh and Ephraim...And Jacob said...and now thy two sons, Ephraim and Manasseh, which were born unto thee in the land of Egypt before I came unto thee into Egypt, are MINE; as Reuben and Simeon, they shall be mine...And Israel beheld Joseph's sons and said, who are these? And Joseph said unto his father, they are my sons, whom God hath given me in this place. And he said, Bring them unto me, and I shall bless them. Now the eyes of Israel were dim for age, so that he could not see. And he brought them near unto him; and he kissed them and embraced them...The Angel which redeemed me from all evil, bless the lads; and let thy name be named on them, and the name of my father's Abraham and Isaac...And he blessed them that day, saying, In thee shall Israel bless, saying, God make thee as Ephraim and as Manasseh" (Genesis 48:1–28).

Notice the words of the patriarch: "and now thy two sons...are mine, as Reuben and Simeon, they shall be mine" (Verse 5). And also notice the words of Joseph himself: "They are my sons, *whom God hath given me in this place.*" The heart of the aged patriarch warmed towards his negroid grandsons, for he blessed them as fellows: "The Angel who delivered me from all evil, bless the lads"...and let my name be named on them, etc. But this seemed not enough for Israel, for he added: "In thee shall Israel bless, saying, God make thee as Ephraim and Manasseh." These striking passages need no further comment. They contain much food for serious thought to those who are prayerfully seeking a solution of the so-called 'Negro Problem,' especially among the ever-increasing ranks of Bible students.[31]

"Manasseh, the first child, although he was born in a Black Kingdom, Black Manasseh and his descendants would be known as Hebrews. The house of Manasseh would suffer the slavery and experience the liberation of the Hebrews.

Like Black Manasseh, Black Ephraim was a strong baby boy. In the story of the birth of Black Ephraim is a profound Black Revelation. Joseph did not bow down to the evils of a system that tried to compel him to have affairs with Potiphar's wife in order to maintain his position in the Black system. Joseph did that which was righteous. Black people—men and women—in this American system that pushes them toward evil should do that which is righteousness—right in God's eyesight.

Joseph was made to suffer for doing right. Black Adams will be made to suffer; however, God will not allow you to suffer forever. The history of the Black man in America affirms this revelation. Only after the Black people had lived righteously in the oppressive system and had suffered for a short period did God initiate His elevation of Black people in the oppressive American system."[32]

"The beautiful Asenath was a member of a pure black African race which intermixed its seed among the free and enslaved Hebrews. The Israelites, before and after the Exodus, were definitely black-skinned and biracial. The Greek historian and geographer Strabo (63 B.C. – 24 A.D.) said that during his lifetime, it was not unusual for historians to think that Jews were of Negro ancestry. Strabo went on to say that Jews living in western Judea were mixed with African blood.

The modern day Egyptians, who are largely composed of European blood (fifty percent), are descendants from an ancient Black-Negro race. Their forefather (ancestor) was a Negro called Mizraim, meaning Egypt (Genesis 10:6)."[33] From these black people who greatly mattered to God, came much of the literature, science

Black Women in the Bible – Old Testament

and inventions that greatly influenced what is referred to as modern society.

---

1. Lockyer, Herbert. *All the Women of the Bible*, p. 168.
2. Woolsey, Raymond H. *Men and Women of Color in the Bible*, p. 35.
3. Johnson, John L. *The Black Biblical Heritage*, p. 71.
4. Woolsey, Raymond H. *Men and Women of Color in the Bible*, p. 33–35.
5. Rhoades, F.S. *Black Characters and References of the Holy Bible*, p.25, 26.
6. Woolsey, Raymond H. *Men and Women of Color in the Bible*, p. 36, 37.
7. Holly, Alonzo Potter. *God and the Negro*, p. 59.
8. *Ibid*. p. 60, 61.
9. Woolsey, Raymond H. *Men and Women of Color in the Bible*, p. 37.
10. Unger, Merrill F. *Unger's Bible Dictionary*, p. 736.
11. Woolsey, Raymond H. *Men and Women of Color in the Bible*, p. 23.
12. Lockyer, Herbert. *All the Women of the Bible*, p. 82.
13. Unger, Merrill F. *Unger's Bible Dictionary*, p. 737
14. Lockyer, Herbert. *All the Women of the Bible*, p. 61.
15. Rhoades, F. S. *Black Characters and References of the Holy Bible*, p. 16.
16. Woolsey, Raymond H. *Men and Women of Color in the Bible*, p. 19.
17. *Ibid*. p. 19–21.
18. Holly, Alonzo Potter. *God and the Negro*, p. 47–51.
19. Woolsey, Raymond H. *Men and Women of Color in the Bible*, p. 21.
20. Lockyer, Herbert. *All the Women of the Bible*, p. 31, 32.
21. Unger, Merrill F. *Unger's Bible Dictionary*, p. 112
22. Lockyer, Herbert. *All the Women of the Bible*, p. 32.
23. Woolsey, Raymond H. *Men and Women of Color in the Bible*, p. 27, 29.
24. Rhoades, F. S. *Black Characters and References of the Holy Bible*, p. 17.
25. Woolsey, Raymond H. *Men and Women of Color in the Bible*, p. 29.
26. Rhoades, F. S. *Black Characters and References of the Holy Bible*, p. 17, 18.
27. Woolsey, F. S. *Men and Women of Color in the Bible*, p. 29.
28. Lockyer, Herbert. *All the Women of the Bible*, p. 32.
29. Holly, Alonzo Potter. *God and the Negro*, p. 44.
30. *King James Version of the Bible (The)*
31. Holly, Alonzo Potter. *God and the Negro*, p. 44–46.
32. Rhoades, F. S. *Black Characters and References of the Holy Bible*, p. 18, 19.
33. Johnson, John L. *The Black Biblical Heritage*, p. 59.

CHAPTER 10

Summary

I purposed to do this book essentially from the biblical references and notes that I had gathered over several years, along with some help from Bible dictionaries and commentaries that would substantiate my study conclusions. However, I later decided to read more reference books about the characters from Scripture that I was presenting from my research to see what others had written.

I was amazed to see the prejudiced slant in religious academia concerning apparent black characters in Scripture. That slant seemed to always present these people of color, especially black, with negative connotations. Many of the white scholars would point out undesirable traits and overlook the plethora of positive virtues. No character will be perfect in entirety because only one person, Jesus Christ, fits that category. However, there was the relentless tendency to focus on the negative qualities of black characters, even to the point of overlooking apparent pristine qualities.

Beyond that, many white authors in the Western Hemisphere of the religious world refused to acknowledge many apparent characters as being a person of color, though historically some had been accepted that way. Some commentaries would even go overboard to reject the obvious fact that a particular character was black or a

Summary

person of color. This attitude is ludicrous when you consider that 80 to 90% of the world are people of color. How could you expect the Bible to be void of those percentages?

Some Bible dictionaries in a common presentation of facts and truth would prove that a certain character was black, and then put a footnote or comment saying that these facts don't mean that the person was black like the Negro of the United States. Again, the desire to disprove what was already proved by them was ridiculous.

Overall it was a delight to write this book. Much of my research was expanded by some writers. I enjoyed seeing characters that had been hidden by most Bible readers come alive in their perceptions and thinking as I shared parts of this book with them. Many preachers immediately wanted to take notes to preach a sermon on characters they had read about all their life but had not seen who they really are.

I watched educated people who regularly study the Bible repent of their prejudices and narrow vision. I had people say they were sorry to me because they had not separated the indoctrinations of society in the United States and the Western Hemisphere from a true study of the Scriptures.

If this kind of response is genuine and sincere, then I have accomplished my goal in writing this book and doing this research. If I can help people to know the truth – see the truth – accept the truth – and be changed by the truth, then, I am most gratified.

I am hoping that Christian academia will take these discoveries and facts seriously and will adjust their curriculum to be fair and void of the traditional prejudice of presenting black people as inferior just because of the color of their skin. Racism and religion have always been partners in marring the image of God to benefit those in power. Many missionaries went to countries of dark-skinned people and said their noses were wrong, their lips were wrong, their rhythm was wrong, and their dance was wrong, to make the people feel inferior. Then they presented a blonde-haired, blue-eyed image of Jesus (Michael Angelo's uncle), and said you have to be like this to worship God correctly. Afterward, it was easy for the colonialist to come in and enslave a people who lost their sense of identity and self-worth through missionaries and religious teaching that was prejudiced against blacks. Why? Because religion had already bound their spirit, and when your spirit is bound, it is very easy to come and bind you economically, educationally, socially, sexually, emotionally, and then physically.

"You shall know the truth, and the truth shall make you free" (John 8:32). The word *free* and *make* are the same Greek word. It means:

1) The truth shall liberate you and exempt you from moral liability – that is freedom from the effects of systems or society.
2) The truth shall liberate you and exempt you from ceremonial liability – that is freedom from religion.
3) The truth shall liberate you or exempt you from mortal liability – that is from man or mankind (or in slang vernacular, we say, 'keeping up with the Jones').

In conclusion, my hope is that we truly have a revival or reformation of truth in the Body of Christ in this generation. May this revival or reformation help to break down the walls of racial prejudice, gender prejudice, national prejudice and any other prejudices. Then, may we live the reality of Jesus' new commandment to "Love one another as I have loved you" and may we start to be recognized as His disciples by our 'love for one another." Now you can answer for yourself, "Do Black Lives Matter to God?"

About The Author

Reverend Dr. Jefferson Edwards is Founder and Senior Pastor of the Freedom Christian Center Church in Kansas City, Missouri, and the President of Jeff Edwards Ministries International. For over 42 years he has traveled extensively as an itinerant minister across the United States and to more than 15 nations.

Dr. Edwards has had the privilege of addressing many Prime Ministers and Representatives of Government in these locations. He is the author of the best-selling book, *Chosen—Not Cursed*. Among his other books are *Liberated—No Longer Bound, The Call of God, Gifted—Discovering Your Hidden Greatness, Purging Racism From Christianity,* and *Where Are All The Fathers?*

Dr. Edwards has a special commission and mandate from God to bring down the barriers that divide races and denominations. He addresses the present day crisis concerning the family with a particular emphasis on black men, and the black family. With a Bachelors and Masters degrees in Biblical Theology and a Ph.D. in Biblical and Ethnical Studies (the study of races and people groups in the Bible), Dr. Edwards developed curriculum for this major. He completed his doctoral dissertation on the subject of Biblical Black History and also received an honorary Doctor of Divinity degree.

Regarded as a gifted preacher, teacher, and prophet to churches in the United States, Dr. Jefferson Edwards is recognized as an Apostle to the Nations and the Body of Christ.

Please visit his website www.jeffedwards.org.

Bibliography

Clarke, Adam. *Adam Clark's Commentary, Electronic Database,* Biblesoft, Inc., 2006.

Comparative Study Bible (The), Grand Rapids: Zondervan Bible Publishers, 1984, Reprinted, 1986.

Dictionary.com, Unabridged, Based on the Random House Dictionary, Random House, Inc., 2011.

Halley, Henry M. *Halley's Bible Handbook,* Grand Rapids: Zondervan Publishing House, 1965.

Holly, Alonzo Potter. *God and the Negro,* Nashville: National Baptist Publishing Board, 1937.

Hyman, Mark. *Blacks Who Died for Jesus,* Philadelphia: Corrective Black History Books, 1983.

International Bible Dictionary (The), Plainfield: Logos International, 1977.

Jamieson, Robert, A. R. Fauset, and David Brown. *A Commentary on the Old and New Testaments,* Grand Rapids: Zondervan Publishing House, 1966.

Johnson, John L. *Black Biblical Heritage, (The),* Nashville: Winston-Derek Publishers, 1991.

King James Version of the Bible (The), Thomas Nelson Publishers.

Lockyer, Herbert. *All the Men of the Bible,* Grand Rapids: Zondervan Publishing House, 1958.

Lockyer, Herbert. *All the Women of the Bible*, Grand Rapids: Zondervan Publishing House, 1967.

McCray, Walter Arthur. *Black Presence in the Bible, (The)*, Chicago: Black Light Fellowship, 1989.

New Lexicon Webster's Dictionary of the English Language, New York: Lexicon Publications, Inc., 1989 Edition.

Orr, James. *The International Standard Bible Encyclopedia, Volume IV*, Grand Rapids: Wm. B. Eerdmans Publishing Co., 1956, Reprinted 1996.

Orr, James. *The International Standard Bible Encyclopedia, Volume II*, Grand Rapids: Wm. B. Eerdmans Publishing Co., 1956, Reprinted 1996.

Revised Standard Version of the Bible (The).

Rhoades, F. S. *Black Characters and References of the Holy Bible*, New York: Vantage Press, Inc., 1980.

Rogers, J. A. *100 Amazing Facts About the Negro, With Complete Proof*, New York: Futuro Press, Inc., 1957.

Strong, James H. *Strong's Exhaustive Concordance*, Grand Rapids: Baker Book House, Reprint, 1985.

Unger, Merrill F. *New Unger's Bible Dictionary, (The)*, Chicago: Moody Press, 1988.

Vine, W. E. & F. F. Bruce. *Vine's Expository Dictionary of the Old and New Testament Words*, Old Tappan: Fleming H. Ravell Company, 1981.

Whiston, William. *The Life and Work of Flavius Josephus*, 1981.

Woolsey, Raymond H. *Men and Women of Color in the Bible*, Langley Park: International Bible, Inc., 1977.

Suggested Reading

Bennett, Jr., Lerone. *Before The Mayflower*, Chicago: Johnson Publishing Company, 1976.

Custance, Arthur C. *Noah's Three Sons*, Grand Rapids: Zondervan Publishing Company, 1975.

Edwards, Jefferson D. *Chosen – Not Cursed!*, Tulsa: Vincom, 1989.

Edwards, Jefferson D. *Gifted – Discovering Your Hidden Greatness*, Bakersfield: Pneuma Life Publishing, 1994.

Edwards, Jefferson D. *Purging Racism From Christianity*, Grand Rapids: Zondervan Publishing House, 1996.

Holly, Alonzo Potter. *God and the Negro*, Nashville: National Baptist Publishing Board, 1937.

McCray, Walter Arthur. *The Black Presence in the Bible*, Chicago: Black Light Fellowship, 1989.

McKissic, William Dwight. *Beyond Roots: In Search of Blacks in the Bible*, Wenonah: Renaissance Productions, 1990.

Mosely, William. *What Color Was Jesus*, Chicago: African American Images, 1987.

Rogers, J. A. *100 Amazing Facts About the Negro with Complete Proof*, New York: J. A. Rogers, 1957.

Rogers, J. A. *Sex and Race, 3 Volumes*, St. Petersburg: Helga M. Rogers, 1967.

www.ingramcontent.com/pod-product-compliance
Lightning Source LLC
Chambersburg PA
CBHW051654040426
42446CB00009B/1138